KOOS
BEKKER'S
BILLIONS

KOOS
BEKKER'S
BILLIONS

T.J. STRYDOM

Enjoy the read!

TJ

PENGUIN BOOKS

Koos Bekker's Billions
Published by Penguin Random House (Pty) Ltd
Company Reg. No. 1953/000441/07
The Estuaries No. 4, Oxbow Crescent, Century Avenue,
Century City, Cape Town, 7441
www.penguinrandomhouse.co.za

Penguin
Random House
South Africa

First published 2022
Reprinted before publication

3 5 7 9 10 8 6 4 2

PUBLISHER: Marlene Fryer
COMMISSIONING EDITOR: Marida Fitzpatrick
MANAGING EDITOR: Louis Gaigher
EDITOR: Riaan de Villiers
PROOFREADER: Lisa Compton
COVER DESIGN: Ryan Africa
TEXT DESIGN/TYPESETTER: Natascha Olivier

Set in 10 pt on 16.5 pt Charter

Printed by **novus print**, a division of Novus Holdings

MIX
Paper from
responsible sources
FSC
www.fsc.org   FSC® C022948

ISBN 978-1-77609-657-2 (print)
ISBN 978-1-77609-658-9 (ePub)

For Lejanie

CONTENTS

CONTENTS

PREFACE

I N 1970, A SCHOOLBOY CLAIMED VICTORY OVER AN ESTABLISHED part of South Africa's entertainment industry. Strangely, judging by his reputation later in life, Jacobus Petrus Bekker used an old medium to outmanoeuvre a newer one.

The battle for eyeballs took place in Heidelberg, a town some fifty kilometres south-east of Johannesburg, where Bekker, known to all as Koos, was his school's best speaker and chair of the debating society. In a bid to rejuvenate public discourse at the Hoër Volkskool, his committee livened up their events by making discussions more topical, pushing a few of the 'shy guys' to pitch in and limiting musical interludes to only the best, wrote Bekker in the 1970 yearbook.

The result: well-attended debates, a willingness to participate and an enthusiastic audience. 'Even the allure of slipping out to the drive-in theatre during debating evenings seems to be dying a natural death,' Bekker boasted.

A case of 'debating killed the movie star'? Probably not. The knife fight scene in *Butch Cassidy and the Sundance Kid*, which came out that same year, can't be beaten for entertainment value, certainly not by a few teenagers' speeches.

More likely the young man just grasped early on how to put the best spin on results when delivering an annual report to stakeholders. And he was not wrong about the imminent death of the drive-in ... movie magic would find a new parking spot in the decades that followed.

The name 'Koos' is probably best translated as 'Jack'. At school, Bekker was a bit of a Koos of all trades. He played in the first cricket team, won the regional trophy as part of the first tennis team and even led the second rugby team to victory in its league that year.

And he was clever to boot – the dux pupil who passed Afrikaans, English, Mathematics and Physical Science with distinction. Sure, it was not quite the seven As clocked up by future Constitutional Court justice Edwin Cameron that year. But fewer than hundred matriculants in the entire Transvaal, then South Africa's most populous province, scored four distinctions or more in those final exams.

Of course, he was head boy too. And head prefects get to say their farewells. 'And whatever each of us might accomplish, it will not only be a personal achievement, but an achievement in which the Heidelberg Volkskool also had a stake,' were Bekker's parting words.[1]

In this case, it turned out to be a stake worth a tidy sum half a century later. Page to a footnote below the chair's remuneration for 2020 in the Naspers annual report, and the fine print reads: 'Koos Bekker elected to donate the rand equivalent of his director's fees, being R2,1m (pre-tax), to education. This year the recipient was the Hoër Volkskool in Heidelberg.'

Who can afford to pass on a R2,1 million pay cheque? A dollar billionaire, that's who.

'I'm not convinced that great wealth is really correlated to happiness,' Bekker told a room of MBA graduates in the Netherlands in 2014.

'When you make the first few million euros, it's going to change your life totally. You can look after your parents, you can eat in any restaurant in the world, you can travel for a holiday ... it gives you liberty.'

He himself used that freedom to build a career that brought him even bigger financial rewards. 'So, the first million is very important, but then there is a diminishing return. Between 10 million euros and 100 million, nothing much happens. Between 100 million and 200 million, absolutely nothing happens, right?' he said.

It was a spunky speech to deliver to an auditorium full of MBAs. Most of the eyes in the room had already glazed over with dollar, euro or renminbi signs.

'Beyond a certain point, money is pretty pointless and certainly not worth devoting your life to,' he added.[2]

It's always tough to accurately gauge the means of the truly wealthy, and 'rich lists' do a fair bit of guessing. In January 2022, *Forbes* estimated Bekker's fortune at $2,8 billion, and ranked him the 1008th richest person in the world.[3]

Even if you ignore his property portfolio and the mountains of cash he raked in with share sales over the years, it still adds up to a bundle. Making the most conservative of estimates, looking only at his publicly listed stock in Cape Town-based Naspers and Amsterdam-listed Prosus will get you to R16 billion (more than $1 billion) in early 2022. As his source of wealth, *Forbes* lists 'media, investments, self-made'.

So something happened between 1970 and 2020. Bekker dabbled in media and investments and made himself billions. But how? What did a boy who grew up on a mealie farm do to build such a fortune?

In the first decade or so, his approach seems quite ordinary. Bekker studied languages, law and literature at Stellenbosch University, dabbled in student journalism and met his future wife, Karen Roos. He then moved to the north and, while doing an LLB at Wits University, he had his introduction to the business of television, filling in as translator for the dubbing of dramas and documentaries.[4] He tried his hand at being a state prosecutor, but soon quit. Next, he worked in advertising.

In the meantime he married Karen, who became one of the nation's first television presenters. By the early 1980s, with South Africa descending into violence in apartheid's deadly final decade, they had decided to leave the country.

He sold his house and borrowed as much as he could to enrol for an MBA at Columbia University in New York. 'I went to America to go and work there,' he recounted later. 'I did not want to come back. It was the 1980s, and South Africa looked quite grim.'[5]

A few years later, however, he did return to start a pay-TV company soon to be known as M-Net. When it became profitable, Bekker took the concept to Europe, where he stitched together a business that spanned more than a dozen countries on the continent, selling it for a tidy profit a few years later.

M-Net was only the first of the so-called M-group of companies he founded. The others – MIH, MTN and M-Web – each became what could have been a decent success story for any entrepreneur. Bekker took it to another level.

In 1997, he settled in Cape Town and became CEO of Nasionale Pers. This is where he found and assembled all the ingredients he needed to make (or bake) billions.

'I think "recipes", like "principles", are dangerous. Both imply a certain timelessness to your outlook, a rock-solid truth you were born with and with which you will die,' he told Ebbe Dommisse in an interview for the latter's book *Fortunes: The rise and rise of Afrikaner tycoons.*[6]

Perhaps Bekker did not follow a recipe from the start, but he definitely cooked up something. And a study of his life and career reveals some incredibly useful kitchen habits.

His approach was a clever combination of reading the wind, throwing caution to the wind and embracing the winds of change. Over more than four decades he used several methods to give him the best chance of making it big. This book distills these to fifteen strategies. If you like, call it the 'how to make billions' listicle (number ten will shock you!). The first is: Get paid like an entrepreneur.

1.

GET PAID LIKE
AN ENTREPRENEUR

'Show me the money. Show ... me ... the ... money!'
    – A FAMOUS LINE FROM *JERRY MAGUIRE*

'A gun to the head concentrates the mind admirably.'
    – KOOS BEKKER ON HIS REMUNERATION, 2015[1]

PETS WENT DIGITAL WITH THE TAMAGOTCHI. WITHIN MONTHS, millions of children – and their parents – were making sure the pixelated creature that had hatched on the screen of a small egg-shaped Japanese device would not become hungry or feel unhappy. Half a day's neglect could make the difference between digital life and death.

Just like the Macarena and the movie *Jerry Maguire*, Tamagotchis hit South Africa in the same year that Koos Bekker and Ton Vosloo had their billion-dollar chat.

'So I said, all right, I'll come, but I don't want a salary or a bonus or a car or a medical scheme or anything like that,' Bekker told an interviewer later in life.[2] The job on offer was Vosloo's, as CEO of Naspers. The starting date was 1 October 1997.

Naspers executives reach retirement age at sixty. Vosloo, a life-long newspaperman, was not going to miss a deadline by much, so he stepped down one day after his sixtieth birthday, and was ready to slot into the role of non-executive chair.

'In my own mind I had already picked Bekker as my successor years earlier; in my opinion, there was no one in the Nasionale Pers group, or in our entire media industry, who was better suited to the task of leading the company,' Vosloo wrote in his memoirs, published in 2018.[3]

He quipped that his successor's last role in print media had been in 1974 as editor of the Stellenbosch student newspaper *Die Matie*. But the Koos Bekker of 1997 was hardly an inexperienced executive. He had been running M-Net since the mid-1980s, and had spent most of the 1990s in the Netherlands stringing together a European pay-TV empire. But a massive deal he had lined up with an American giant did not go through, and his company was merged with a French pay-TV business called Canal Plus (Canal+).

Bekker was offered a senior position with Canal+'s international operations, but for him this was never an option.[4] And who would want to work somewhere in the belly of a European business if in Cape Town he could get everything he had asked for?

'I don't want a fixed package, and you can fire me on 24 hours' notice,' Bekker told Vosloo. But he added: 'I want 3 per cent of the long-term value created above inflation.'[5]

The notion of incentivising executives with share allotments had gained traction since the mid-1970s, when the American economists Michael Jensen and William Meckling published an academic paper about the behaviour of managers in companies.[6] Jensen later recommended stock options as the surest way to get executives to do the things that would maximize value for shareholders.[7] This basically means giving the CEO the option of buying his or her company's shares at the current price, but on a predetermined date in the future.

The idea was not new in South Africa, or even at Naspers – the company had been running a share incentive trust for senior management since 1987. But it wasn't nearly as popular as on Wall Street. By the time

Bekker cut his deal with Vosloo and Naspers, rewarding executives with share options was all the rage in the United States.

In 1993 the US Congress passed legislation that made this method of remuneration more cost-effective.[8] Then the floodgates opened. Two decades later, critics blame everything from the Enron corporate governance scandal to the 2007/8 global financial crisis on incentives for CEOs to maximise shareholder value. But in the right circumstances, says Bekker, it can provide a 'wonderful alignment of interests'.[9]

Most company bosses take a salary and performance bonus and then negotiate stock options as a kicker. But Bekker kept it much simpler than that. He just went all in.

'So, we start on a certain day, and then there is a value, and then we measure it again after five years. And we say, if the value is only that, or only that plus inflation, then you take home nothing,' went his conversation with Vosloo.[10]

At that time, Naspers had a market capitalisation of about R6 billion, and the inflation rate was nearly 10 per cent. If Bekker wanted to earn anything at all in the five years that followed, he had to get Naspers to a market cap of more than R9 billion by the end of 2002. Challenge accepted!

'That's the trade-off ... that you say, okay, give me a generous share allowance, and I'll basically act as a co-owner and not as an employee. And I will take the risks that come with it,' Bekker explained in 2015.[11]

And generous it was. By 1996, the entire board, including Vosloo, who had served as chief executive since 1984, held a mere 1,18 per cent of the company's issued share capital.[12] And here the new guy was asking for nearly 3 per cent.

Luckily for him, Naspers was ideally suited to this arrangement. The share incentive trust for senior management had already been in operation for a decade. Moreover, Naspers had ten times more shares available to award to executives than before it listed on the JSE in 1994.

When Bekker took the reins, the company's board had more than 11 million shares – nearly 10 per cent of the company – at its disposal for this purpose. So Bekker took the job. The board of directors recommended a five-year contract, and shareholders approved it.

'It remains to be seen whether you should be offering me congratulations or commiseration,' Bekker quipped in an interview after his appointment.[13]

When he retired as CEO seventeen years later, congratulations were certainly in order. Naspers had grown from its R6 billion market cap to more than R530 billion. And Bekker held nearly 16,4 million shares worth more than R1 000 each. An impressive haul, comfortably making him a dollar billionaire.

During his tenure, Naspers made a number of bad investments, a few mediocre ones, a few good ones and one that shot the lights out. The stake Bekker and his team bought in 2001 in the Chinese technology firm Tencent outperformed everything else, and was one of the best technology investments of the twenty-first century.

Thanks to his initial deal with Vosloo, Bekker was in a position to reap the full reward. He got paid not as a regular CEO, but like an entrepreneur.

'Because you think as an owner, you don't think as an employee,' he commented later. 'So you don't say, I want to stay in a good hotel, or how could I improve my bonus? There *is* no bloody bonus.'[14]

But it wasn't all plain sailing. Bekker's career coincided with monumental shifts in the way people communicate, socialise and transact. Television, mobile phones and the internet upended entire industries by making established services faster, more convenient or even free. And the transformation brought with it big booms and sudden busts. Bekker calls the internet, which was first commercialised in 1995, the biggest development of his lifetime.

'When the internet started, I completely underestimated it,' he told an interviewer in 2016. 'Only by about 1997 did we realise, here is something really big.'[15] And by then, he was the CEO of a listed company with money to allocate to new ventures.

So, in the late 1990s Bekker pivoted the company towards technology, and specifically the internet. Naspers spent hundreds of millions of rands on bedding down the infrastructure for internet service providers such as

M-Web, not only in South Africa but also in places such as Thailand, Indonesia and China.

Through its MIH subsidiary, run by Bekker's long-time friend Cobus Stofberg, Naspers invested in the software supplier Mindport, and took a punt on an interactive television business called OpenTV.

New uses for the internet and its rapid adoption in many parts of the world led to a digital gold rush. The founders of companies with hardly any revenue, and rarely turning a profit, sprinted to list their businesses on New York's Nasdaq exchange, a favourite among technology investors. In the euphoria, the bourse's composite index, its main measure of the value of listed shares, rose from less than 1 000 points in 1995 to more than 5 000 early in 2000.

In the same year, Microsoft climbed to a market cap that made it ten times more valuable than the world's largest car maker, General Motors.

Eventual giants eBay, Yahoo! and Amazon also made their debut in those heady days, but others such as Globe.com, reckoned by some to be the first social network, fizzled within a couple of years of listing. In the midst of all this activity, Bekker was also eager to tap international markets for a piece of the action.

And so, in 1999, Naspers listed MIH on the Nasdaq and in Amsterdam to expand its internet operations, develop international services and extend pay-TV's push into foreign markets.[16] Later that year, OpenTV was also floated on the Nasdaq and in Amsterdam (more in chapter 7).

'Luckily, we didn't buy assets at silly prices during the bubble, but we got ourselves into several money-losing developments,' Bekker told Anton Harber, author of *Gorilla in the Room: Koos Bekker and the rise and rise of Naspers*, published in 2012.[17]

And there were many silly prices going around. In 2000, for example, the search engine America Online (AOL) concluded a mega-merger with the media conglomerate Time Warner, in a deal valued at $350 billion.[18] The monster that emerged started reporting losses the very next year, and never lived up to expectations.

Unrealistic valuations had formed a market bubble that popped spectacularly in what became known as the dotcom crash.

The Nasdaq peaked in March of that year. Then a few weeks of bad news unnerved investors: Japan, the world's second-largest economy, slid into a recession; Microsoft was slapped with a multibillion-dollar fine for anti-competitive behaviour; and the US Federal Reserve raised interest rates. As soon as sentiment turned negative, the sell-off became self-sustaining. Every snippet of unfavourable news pummelled tech stocks further.

Microsoft's share price, for example, nosedived from nearly $60 to barely $20 in twelve months. It took the company sixteen years to get back to the level its stock was trading at before the crash.

And the shock waves reverberated all the way to the southern tip of Africa. When, in October 2000, Bekker called the internet 'fundamentally useful – we just need to find a way to make money from it', he would have had good reason to update his CV and start speaking to recruiters. Shareholders don't have a sense of humour when the value of their portfolios begin shrinking.[19]

On Bekker's first day as CEO, Naspers shares traded at about R32. In the deepest trough after the dotcom crash, they were languishing at R12, and the company had a market cap of only R2 billion. Bekker reported a loss of R1,9 billion to shareholders in 2002, down from a profit of R1 billion in 2001 and a long way off the R3,3 billion netted in 2000. Far from creating value, in his first four years on the job Bekker had actually overseen a two-thirds decline.

And there was no quick recovery. Investor sentiment had turned against technology businesses, especially where there was even a whiff of an over-optimistic profit promise. In 2002, by the time Bekker should have been rubbing his hands for a big payday, the share price was still far below the level when he took the reins. He got nothing.

'From a personal point of view, the risk is high,' he said in 2015. 'Unless you've made some money early in life that can tide you over if things go wrong, you can actually land up in financial difficulties.'[20]

Not earning a cent for five years' work? Financial difficulties are an understatement. Especially if you consider it was the half-decade between ages forty-five and fifty, a time when many professionals really start raking it in.

But Bekker had no intention of being paid like a professional. Even though he had an office job at an established company, he was after the hits and misses of an entrepreneur. Fortunately, he had the backing to hold on to his position – and a personal war chest. 'I was lucky, I made money at the age of thirty, and then I made more money at forty,' he said in a speech in 2014.[21]

His earlier success with M-Net and the windfall it brought after listing in 1990, as well as a tidy sum he had made in establishing MTN, allowed Bekker to stick around long enough for his investment strategy to bear fruit.

Bekker had what *Black Swan* author Nassim Taleb colourfully calls 'fuck you money'. It's not a specific amount, but enough to chase your dreams. 'So when you're sitting in the bath, you remind yourself: it doesn't matter what the share price is tomorrow evening, but it does matter a great deal what it's at five years hence,' reflected Bekker in 2015.[22]

For the first few years of his tenure, Naspers annual reports were cryptic about its deal with Bekker – the company only published details of the CEO's remuneration in 2002. In this year, it concluded a new contract with him, basically on the same terms.

The tide turned, and over the next five years Bekker made a bundle. Then he went on a year-long sabbatical and returned for a final stint. From 2010 onwards, Naspers's share price truly rocketed – and Bekker pocketed 3 per cent of that rally.

During more than a decade and a half at the helm, he benefitted like an entrepreneur, but was fortunate in having to deal with fewer of the pitfalls.

Though his leap of faith as unpaid Naspers CEO came with 'no fall-back and no parachute', many entrepreneurs jump while holding an anvil. Bekker invested time. Most other entrepreneurs pile in all their own funds and everything they can borrow from all those who would lend to them.[23]

Amazon founder Jeff Bezos sourced the start-up capital for what would become the world's largest online retailer primarily from his parents. '[They] invested a large fraction of their life savings in something they didn't understand. They weren't making a bet on Amazon or the concept of a bookstore on the internet. They were making a bet on their son,' he recounted in 2020.[24]

Bezos told them he thought there was a 70 per cent chance they would lose their investment, but they still backed him.

Likewise, Nike founder Phil Knight funded his first shoe imports from Japan with a loan from his father. In his memoir, *Shoe Dog,* he gives a thrilling account of the cash-flow struggles he endured during his first decade in business, and how he was often at the mercy of financial institutions and his own creditors.

At Naspers, Bekker was free from the month-to-month worries of other entrepreneurs that they might not be able to pay salaries. There is also no public record of Bekker ever signing personal surety for a Naspers transaction – yet that is what Knight had to do several times.

A South African example would be Christo Wiese convincing his father in the mid-1960s to sell his business and invest in Pep Stores.

For most entrepreneurs, raising capital starts at home. Then they hit the road. 'It took more than 50 meetings for me to raise $1 million from investors,' says Bezos.[25] And finding investors that aren't only interested in the business model but are also satisfied with the timelines and the management can be tough.

Bekker certainly did some heavy footwork when raising the funds to establish M-Net, but when he created the lion's share of his wealth from 1997 onwards, he had no need to convince investors of the merits of setting up a new company. Naspers was already there, and had been in business for eight decades.

Importantly, the company had existing relationships with investors, banks and other financial institutions. It had established corporate governance procedures, and was even listed on the JSE. Financing the day-today running of the business or tapping the market for funds to expand was nothing new.

So Bekker walked into a useful structure. Even though he then set about reshaping it (more in chapter 4), he did not have to put in months of effort to build the business from scratch.

A further benefit of Bekker's unusual deal with Naspers was that he avoided some of the difficulties the founder of a business often grapples with. Though he made a fortune, his stake in the company remained modest compared to other investors. When he retired as CEO, Bekker was not even close to holding the largest stake in Naspers. The Public Investment Corporation held nearly 15 per cent of the company, and Bekker less than 3 per cent.

Many founders, such as Facebook's Mark Zuckerberg, remain the largest shareholders in the enterprises they started. At the beginning of 2022, Zuckerberg still held 13 per cent of Meta Platforms, which owns Facebook, Instagram and WhatsApp, and Bezos, with 10 per cent, had the biggest stake in Amazon.

Having the most shares in the company you run differs from just being a substantial shareholder, as it attracts much closer scrutiny. Other stakeholders, such as employees, trade unions, the media, regulators and government, sometimes view such a CEO as an outright owner and often as a proxy for the company.

Bekker also avoided the agonising decisions founders face when bringing new investors into a start-up. Very few self-made billionaires got there without gradually letting go of equity to fund business growth. But when to sell shares or issue new ones, and to which partners?

Bekker's dilemma was a different one. His Naspers N-shares vested in three tranches over periods of five years, and apart from his first stint as CEO, he exercised his options every single time. In the process he accumulated nearly 20 million shares.

After a decade at the helm, the value of his Naspers shares greatly overshadowed the money he had made in his thirties and forties.

'I think you enjoy your work more if your personal wealth is tied up in the company,' he remarked in 2008. 'Many financial advisers regard that as rather stupid, but at least if one makes a mistake, then the benefit is that you lose your money yourself – you don't have your money lost for you by financial advisers.'[26]

But at some stage, any rational person would diversify his or her holdings. That means selling some stock.

In 2006 Bekker did flog Naspers N-shares for some R74 million, but used the proceeds to secure a bunch of high-voting Naspers A-shares (more in chapter 9). In other words, he exposed himself even further to the company he was running.

When directors sell shares, their dealings are reported on the Stock Exchange News Service (SENS). The idea is to be transparent and to prevent insider trading by board members, as they often have access to privileged information. But other small shareholders can mostly buy and sell without disclosing it to the general public.

Bekker served on the board of Naspers from 1997 until the time of writing in 2022. Non-stop? No, during that quarter of a century he took two sabbaticals.

The first was in 2007, after the end of two five-year stints as Naspers boss. He gave up his board seat, hung up his gloves as CEO and hit the road.

'I was in my mid-fifties, so I decided to take a break and see the world. So I travelled, and I saw 22 countries,' he disclosed in an interview after his return.[27]

Before joining Naspers, he had, of course, run M-Net for a period of twelve years, so he'd been a company boss for more than two decades. Tiring work, without taking a break.

Elizabeth Gilbert's memoir, *Eat, Pray, Love*, came out the year before. Bekker's version was more like browse, teach, leave. He travelled to California, South Korea and Japan, among other places, to observe the cutting edge of media and tech trends. But he also spent time with the Pennsylvania Dutch, better known as the Amish, to see how they function without technology. He even lectured in Mongolia.

Before he set off, he said he hoped to read widely, think and relax – and then return as CEO for a final stint with new energy and ideas. What he didn't say was that he would use the opportunity to offload nearly 1,8 million Naspers shares.

'Well, one has to make a living, so from time to time executives sell shares. I've never been a very keen seller,' he told an interviewer after returning to his desk in April 2008.[28]

During his year on sabbatical, Bekker was not a director, and conveniently the disposal of those shares was not flagged in a SENS statement, but only became public knowledge months later when it was reflected in the company's annual report.

Asked in the same interview about the disclosure of those sorts of deals, he said it was a good thing in general, adding: 'I mean, you might have personal circumstances that force someone to settle – for example, a divorce, or he wants to buy a house or whatever.'[29]

A rather cheeky comment for an executive and board member who has disposed of a mountain of shares, but with other shareholders still in the dark about the transaction.

Get divorced? Buy a house? Bekker chose the latter. That year, he and his wife, Karen, bought Babylonstoren, an expansive estate in the Cape Winelands. The hundreds of millions he pocketed from the share sale came in handy – redeveloping a historic site into a world-class tourist destination does not come cheap.

For his last stint as CEO, Bekker concluded very much the same deal as earlier. Again, no salary, no perks, no golden handshake.

'The sole benefit to Mr Bekker consists of an offer made on the day before assuming duty, i.e. on 31 March 2008, of an option in terms of the rules of the Naspers Limited Share Trust to acquire 11 687 808 Naspers N ordinary shares, which, as before, equals 3 per cent of the company's outstanding shares,' the company announced.[30]

The contract ended early in 2013, just in time for Bekker to hang up his hat at age sixty, in line with Naspers policy. But his retirement plans were put on ice after company veteran Antonie Roux passed away from pancreatic cancer in 2012.

Roux had been CEO of Naspers's internet businesses and was considered a visionary in the consumer internet field. More importantly, he had a strong relationship with the management team at Tencent, the investment that accounted for most of Naspers's stellar growth. He was a safe pair of hands, and without him the company's succession plan hit a wobble.

So Bekker stuck around as CEO for another year – this time, with no compensation whatsoever, not even share options. The company then tapped the former eBay executive Bob van Dijk, who had joined Naspers in 2013 in its Eastern European e-commerce division, as its new chief executive.

'I'm a hands-on type,' Bekker told a television interviewer in 2014, 'so I'm opinionated and obnoxious … and I've been running the company for a long time. So in those circumstances, if you bring a new chap in, he's got almost no chance … It's like coming into Manchester United when Alex Ferguson is still on the board.'[31]

So he followed the same playbook as before and embarked on a sabbatical. He said it was to give his successor a chance to get to know his management team, and bond with the board.

Again, the long-time CEO resigned from the board. The plan was to return as chairman a year later, when Vosloo would relinquish that post.

Again, Bekker was free to sell Naspers stock without having to disclose the transactions on SENS. It was only in the next year's annual report that investors noticed he had disposed of more than two-thirds of his shares. This was just about every share he had earned during his last stint as CEO. Needless to say, some eyebrows changed position from normal to raised.

'Whatever spin the company wants to put on it, it's hard to shake the feeling that selling during the sabbatical was designed so that no details would have to be released to the public,' the veteran journalist Ann Crotty wrote in the *Sunday Times*.[32] And, give or take a billion, Bekker bagged something like R15 billion from the sale.

The new Naspers chair responded that the shares were issued specifically for the CEO role, and that he was no longer CEO.[33] But then why hold on to the rest?

Bekker obviously knew that those shares were poised to make some more impressive gains. Despite the pull-back early in 2022, the value of Naspers stock has more than doubled since he sold so much of it between 2014 and 2015. At the time of writing, in early 2022, he still held nearly 4,7 million shares.

The thing is, if Bekker wanted to buy the shares he had earned in the first place, he needed to exercise the options. And exercising those options had tax implications.

'In no way, given the amounts payable for the original purchase price plus inflation and tax payable, could I afford to take the money from my pocket to exercise the options myself,' he commented in September 2015.[34]

The South African Revenue Service (SARS) did quite well out of the transaction, raking in around R2 billion.

But there is no denying that Bekker's strategy of getting paid like an entrepreneur was as clever a move as corporate South Africa had ever seen.

'And it worked out in the end, but after a lot of pain halfway through. So I don't recommend it, and I don't see many people taking it,' he says.[35]

But to cut that sort of remuneration deal in the first place, you need Bekker's reputation. And to build that reputation, Bekker needed a backer.

2.

EVEN BEKKER NEEDS A BACKER

'Bekker could pull off everything, but with the blessing of
Naspers.'   – TON VOSLOO, 2018[1]

'[I] vaguely wanted to work in the media because I sensed
it was exciting.'   – KOOS BEKKER, 2002[2]

IN HIS FINAL COLUMN AS EDITOR OF *DIE MATIE*, KOOS BEKKER
described the prospects of his university as 'not all that good'.

Stellenbosch was in the platteland and a good thousand miles from
Johannesburg, the country's strongest growth point. This made his alma
mater particularly vulnerable, he wrote in 1975.[3]

If the university failed to offer something truly special, he added, it ran
the risk of turning into a '*boskollege*' (bush college). Quite a parting shot.

Bekker added an honours degree in Afrikaans and Dutch to his BA Law,
got hitched, and together with wife Karen headed for the action up
north. They arrived in the City of Gold just as a new industry was being
born: television.

New for South Africa, that is. Wary of the effect the new medium
would have on the public, the authorities had put it off for as long as
possible. By the time the South African Broadcasting Corporation (SABC)

started with test broadcasts, television services were already running in more than twenty-five other African countries. Bekker had seen it as a nineteen-year-old while hitchhiking through Rhodesia (now Zimbabwe).

'At 24, from an absolute distance, my exposure to it started when Karen, in a fluke, became one of the SABC's first television presenters,' he recounted later.[4] Within a few years – during which he bagged an LLB at the University of the Witwatersrand – they would pull up roots and head for the United States, where TV was big business.

At home, 'the box' had a modest start. When the nationwide service began in January 1976, it consisted of a single channel, and programming was divided relatively equally between English and Afrikaans. The content was just what you would expect from a public broadcaster in apartheid South Africa: ostensibly wholesome, but tightly controlled. Shows curated to toe the National Party (NP) line and catering only for the country's white minority don't make for the best entertainment. Still, South Africans tuned in. Whatever the content, it was TV after all, and the SABC was the only show in town.

Broadcasting was funded, as in the United Kingdom, by means of annual TV licences – but to supplement revenue, two years after the first broadcasts, the SABC started carrying advertisements. Just like that, companies had a new way of reaching consumers nationwide.

The result was a dramatic rearrangement of South Africa's advertising spend. TV blurbs were substantially more expensive to produce, and advertisers splashed out to be on the new medium. The cake was only so big, and it soon became clear that, as more money flowed to TV advertising, less would find its way to the traditional media. Within half a decade, TV's slice had grown from zero to more than a quarter. By the mid-1980s, the SABC, which already had a strong foothold with radio before the advent of TV, was raking in nearly 40 per cent of all advertising.

The SABC was the winner, and print media the loser. The recession that hit South Africa in 1982 made newspapers especially vulnerable, as it meant a contraction in companies' marketing budgets. Businesses tend to buy less advertising space in an economic downturn. And the squeeze was not only on the revenue side – inflation rose to more than 10 per cent, and a weakening rand drove up the cost of newsprint and many other inputs.[5]

The *Rand Daily Mail*, for example, suffered painful losses during this period as a result of the downturn and rapid cost increases. But its owner, South African Associated Newspapers (SAAN), was not the only newspaper group to feel the pinch; others were also reeling. Newspapers were commonly cross-subsidised by other printing ventures. By 1984, only one of four Nasionale Pers newspapers was turning a profit, and the group was carried by its book publishing and magazine divisions.

There was a further threat. Nasionale Pers managing director Ton Vosloo worried that the SABC could start regional TV stations, which would suck even more life out of metropolitan newspapers.[6]

Press bosses coveted a chunk of TV's advertising revenue, and had already expressed interest in sharing a new channel with the state broadcaster. By 1984, the SABC was running three channels, and when a 'TV4' was mooted in parliament as a way of opening up the airwaves to competition, the ears of press rivals Nasionale Pers, SAAN and the Argus Group perked up.

Those groups had already banded together for a minority stake in Radio 702.[7] Some of them had also invested in Bop-TV, a station broadcasting from the nominally independent homeland of Bophuthatswana, now mostly part of North West province, where content was not as tightly controlled as in South Africa itself. The channel soon built up a following in Johannesburg, Soweto and other urban centres within reach of its signal, which it broadcast through the SABC network.

It was a good indication of the appetite for entertaining programming. With the SABC moving to block the signal in affluent areas, it also gave clues as to how strongly the state broadcaster would defend its turf.[8] But just how the press groups could get a piece of the action in South Africa remained uncertain.

That was until Vosloo's phone rang late one afternoon in December 1983. The caller said he was Koos Bekker, an MBA student at Columbia University in New York.[9]

As part of his studies, Bekker had written a paper on pay television. Sure, Home Box Office (HBO) was profitable in the United States with its cable network, but could a similar service be launched elsewhere? His phone pitch to Vosloo: back me to start this business in South Africa, HBO-style, and use the profits to carry your newspapers.

Bekker, then barely thirty, was fortunate to find a press-group boss who was still relatively new in his post. Vosloo, a long-time political journalist and former editor of *Beeld*, was a newspaperman through and through. Nasionale Pers had tapped him for the top job in 1983. He assumed his position in 1984, and was keen to hit the ground running.

'In his first year, the leader has to take big decisions and then submit his proposals, support them with facts and arguments, and get them accepted,' writes Vosloo.[10]

First, he did something approaching a personal due diligence. This consisted of sending his colleague Jan Prins, who was in New York at the time, to look Bekker over. Go for it, Prins reported back. So Vosloo told Bekker to set the idea out in a document. Armed with the memo, Vosloo went to the Naspers board.

A board won't shoot down a recently appointed leader's first ideas without good reason, he says, because 'its members want a leader with a venturesome approach at the helm'.[11] And he was right.

Bekker remembers their first meeting in the Nasionale Pers building on Cape Town's Foreshore late on an April afternoon in 1984. 'I had come from America to sell the concept of M-Net, and a quarter of the way through the presentation the projector jammed,' he recounted later.[12]

After fidgeting with the device, Bekker asked for a pair of scissors – he had once seen someone at an advertising agency get a slide carousel going that way.

At that moment, the meeting was hanging in the balance. The Nasionale Pers top brass shifted around uncomfortably. One of them got up to leave, and said something that gave Bekker the impression he thought it was a waste of time.

'Ton remained seated, in thought. Then he said: "Give him some scissors." The carousel clicked, and two months later we opened a project office in Johannesburg,' Bekker recalled.

Besides the office, Vosloo also got the company to back Bekker with a budget of R50 000, a secretary, and the title of assistant to the managing director.

The young man from New York had to bring the ideas. 'In America I began to realise that pay TV was a new phenomenon that would change the world,' Bekker told an interviewer in 2012.[13]

By the early 1980s, using terrestrial broadcasting technology, even a city the size of New York could only support four channels. Radio waves were used to transmit the signal from a television station to the antenna of each TV set. Reception was often patchy as a nearby building, a passing car or a thunderstorm could interfere with the antenna or the signal.

Cable television opened up new possibilities. It linked homes and broadcasters like plumbing piped water from a dam, and made many more channels possible. As the content travelled along a coaxial cable, there was less interference, and the picture quality was also better and more reliable.

In large cities, the channel options could jump from low single digits to fifty as soon as a cable service had been connected. '[T]he way we watched television started fragmenting into CNN and Disney and, you know, thematic channels,' Bekker recounted.[14]

HBO was a pioneer in pay-TV – it used fresh movies and exclusive sporting events to build a profitable business. Bekker had wanted to work at HBO, and had gone as far as lining up a job at the company. It was one of five positions he was offered in the United States.

But the MBA student also saw a business opportunity. Fragmentation into, say, fifty or one hundred channels creates the opportunity to better understand who the viewers are and how to tailor advertising more closely to their interests. And a monthly subscription fee makes for steady cash flow.

HBO was running such a good business with the backing of media giant Time Inc. that it would be tough to build a competitor in the United States. But why not get publishing groups to fund such a business in another part of the world?

Bekker must have suspected that, with the right backing, he could do better than working nine-to-five, complaining about bosses next to the water cooler, and taking home a decent salary.

He was lucky that Columbia University had one of the world's leading research units on telecommunications and information policy. So he set about collecting every article on pay-TV published anywhere in the English-speaking world – and wrote that paper about trying the business outside the United States. He spent many hours interviewing HBO executives, and got to know their business well.[15]

But cable systems were specific to America, and had been gradually building scale since the late 1940s. The costs of laying down the same sort of infrastructure elsewhere would be prohibitive. There had to be another way of getting a signal to paying viewers only.

'So could you take this technology, encrypt it and send it over the air, and it still works? And after I did the paper, I thought maybe we could. The only country I knew was South Africa, so I came back. I had left South Africa not to come back,' Bekker recalls.[16]

But broadcasting is a tightly regulated industry. And the government of the day ultimately decides who gets to send content over the airwaves. It has the power to grant or deny an all-important broadcasting licence. This is where Bekker needed the man he had phoned from New York.

In Vosloo he had won more than a personal backer. Behind him he also had Nasionale Pers, a large but privately held company with close ties to the government of the day.

Founded in 1915 to publish the Cape Town daily *De Burger* (later *Die Burger*), Nasionale Pers was one leg of the spider that was Afrikaner nationalism. Another was the NP, established only a year earlier by JBM Hertzog as a counterpoint to the governing South African Party, which was loyal to the British Empire.

At the start of the twentieth century, Afrikaners were disgruntled and impoverished after the ravages of the South African War (long called the Anglo-Boer War). When tensions in Europe exploded into World War I, some Afrikaners rebelled against the government's policy of joining the British, French and Russians against Germany and the Austro-Hungarian Empire. They wanted no part in the plan to invade German South West Africa (now Namibia).

The rebels who were arrested and put on trial gained sympathy nation-wide. Soon money was being collected to aid the accused in their defence and to pay fines and damages. And so the Helpmekaarbeweging (Mutual Aid Society) was born. The fundraising campaign was so successful that it became obvious that capital could be mobilised for other causes too.[17]

Soon the short-term insurer Santam, and then the life insurer Sanlam, were established by tapping Afrikaners for capital. Winemakers in the Boland banded together in the KWV, and the demand for funeral policies led to the formation of AVBOB. This all happened within half a decade.

The NP and Nasionale Pers also benefitted. In the slipstream of Afrikaner mobilisation, the former attracted voters, and the latter readers and advertisers.

But it all started with *De Burger*, which was founded to be a mouthpiece of the NP (more in chapter 4). An official alignment of interests between the party and the company remained in place until the 1990s. This proved very useful in 1984.

'The future of the project was entrusted to me. I had to generate the political will on the part of the government to grant us a licence,' writes Vosloo.[18] After spending time as a political journalist in the trenches and among the parliamentary benches, he had existing relationships with many of the big players. As Jan Prins put it later: Vosloo got to know the political VIPs, and they got to know him.[19]

From personal experience, Vosloo remembered that state president PW Botha was an avid newspaper reader; in his distant youth, the *Groot Krokodil* had even done some reporting for Bloemfontein's daily paper. 'I went to him and said, "*Volksblad* has been your favourite over the years, it has carried the NP in the Free State, and if this situation continues with the SABC claiming more and more of the advertising pool, then I will have to start closing newspapers,"' Vosloo recalls.[20]

Volksblad would be one of the first on the chopping board, he told Botha. Packaging the whole deal as a way to protect newspapers against the onslaught of new media was a clever strategy to ensure that the country's political leadership would come on board.

Raising the spectre that the demise of newspapers could affect the party's support also did not hurt: 'You need to remember your political base is those votes on the platteland, where our newspapers have the greatest influence,' he cautioned Botha.

Vosloo also sounded out other party leaders such as Pik Botha, the long-serving minister of foreign affairs, who had broadcasting as a second portfolio. Botha liked the idea of competition for the SABC, but advised Vosloo that he and Bekker should cast the net wider.

'[A]nd I said, it would be tough to convince the cabinet to set up an alternative TV channel (to the SABC) without including the English mainstream media groups,' Botha later told his biographer, Theresa Papenfus.[21]

There was a deeper political rationale. The NP had been gaining votes among English-speaking whites and did not want to be seen to favour the Afrikaans press, Botha later recalled.[22] And Vosloo heard him. 'I went to each proprietor in turn and persuaded them all to join,' he writes.[23]

He stitched together an unlikely partnership of newspaper publishers that was broad enough to satisfy the authorities, but with management control still firmly vested in Nasionale Pers.

The result was an entity in which Nasionale Pers held 26 per cent. The next biggest shareholders were SAAN, Argus and Perskor, with 23 per cent each, while Pietermaritzburg's *Natal Witness* and East London's *Daily Dispatch* held the remainder.[24] The press groups that had only weekly papers missed out.

Now Bekker had a consortium. But even though Nasionale Pers was close to political power, there was still a procedure to be followed.

The government then tasked a group of industry experts with studying the viability of pay-TV, and making recommendations as to who should operate it. At that stage, not only Vosloo and Bekker, and the press groups behind them, were interested in subscription television. More than forty applications were received for the broadcasting licence.

But the real competition lay among three contenders. The first was electronics entrepreneur Bill Venter, founder of Altron, who brought with him the technological know-how, the late Arrie de Beer, a member of the task team, recalled. The second was hotel and casino tycoon Sol Kerzner, who was deemed to know the entertainment industry best. By then, Kerzner also held the movie theatre chain Ster Kinekor in his Satbel group. The press groups, in their consortium called the Electronic Media Network, or M-Net for short, had media experience on their side.[25]

So it was Venter, Kerzner or M-Net. After a round of presentations, which included a memorable one by Bekker (see chapter 5), the task team recommended that the vital licence go to M-Net. Cabinet then approved this, but with strings attached – the channel would not be allowed to broadcast news, for example. 'The National Party's message as conveyed by South Africa's television services had to remain under government control,' Vosloo recalls.[26]

Some years later, the government did offer M-Net the opportunity to carry news broadcasts, but Vosloo declined, remarking that the channel was doing well enough without it, Pik Botha recounted.[27] But that was still a long way off.

So, back to 1985. With the broadcasting licence in the bag, the next step was to tap the press groups for funding. Together they pushed in R60 million, a substantial investment if you consider that it was more than their combined profits the previous year, and that South Africa was mired in a recession.

The economic woes had more than a bit to do with that fan of newspapers PW Botha. His overhyped 'Rubicon Speech' in August that year focused international attention on South Africa's tardy pace of political reform, and sparked the withdrawal of billions of dollars in foreign investment. Economic sanctions also intensified, which meant that South Africa would be a tough environment for anyone planning to set up a new business, especially so for someone who planned on importing technology and buying foreign entertainment.

But a licence and some financing were enough of a start for Bekker to have a go at making the business work.

He was joined by his Stellenbosch University mate Cobus Stofberg, a chartered accountant who had spent some time at the broadcaster CBS in New York, and Jac van der Merwe, head of research and development at Nasionale Pers.[28] 'We needed to get something that would do over the air what cable did on the ground,' Bekker explained in 2002.[29]

In the United States, the infrastructure came all the way into your living room. Remember Jim Carey in *The Cable Guy* saying, 'I'll juice you up!'? It was simply a matter of connecting a cable to the television set. Those who paid were connected and had access to movies and sport; but no cable, no connection, and therefore no exclusive content. To achieve the same with terrestrial broadcasts was a different story.

'So the first focus was, what do we do to scramble a TV picture?' Jock Anderson, transmission manager for M-Net from 1985 to 1993, recalled in a later documentary.[30]

They needed a way to encode an encrypted signal, and broadcast it. Only paying customers should be able to unscramble it. Bekker and his team started to look all over the world. Van der Merwe, with a few colleagues, went scouting.

'We bought a bankrupt little station in America which had developed a certain encryption technology. It was locked up, and the guys had to scale a fence to fetch [software] programs from a derelict building,' remembered Bekker.[31]

In California, the team also came across Oak Technologies, which had just the analogue scrambling technology M-Net needed.[32] Unfortunately, North America used the NTSC system for colour broadcasts, while most of the rest of the world, including South Africa, had adopted PAL.

'We arrived at Oak at a time they had the concepts, they had some American systems working, but nothing that could work in the PAL world,' Anderson recounted.[33] Luckily the business also had laboratories in the Netherlands where Pieter den Toonder, a Dutch engineer who had been doing consulting work for Oak, was developing a European version through his own company, Irdeto.

Den Toonder was in the process of closing down those Oak labs based in Dordtrecht, recalled Antonie Roux, who was part of the technical team.[34] M-Net then purchased the rights, and the Dutch engineer, in the words of Vosloo, 'put the technology to bed for us with his knowledge'.[35]

The South Africans took both the pay-TV subscriber management system and the decoder-encoder technology as is, added Roux.

They then sent engineers to Dordrecht for three months. '[We used] second-hand equipment to put together the basics of a decoding system – the first prototype encoders and decoders,' said Anderson.

The plan was to encode an encrypted signal, broadcast it via the SABC's infrastructure, and supply paying subscribers with a 'black box' that would decode it in turn. The decoders would ensure that there were no freeloaders.

The prototypes were brought back to Johannesburg, and tests over the air proved that the technology was workable. It was a big win. Not having to use cable cut the capital cost of supplying the service to subscribers from billions to less than R100 million, according to Bekker.[36]

But a signal is not worth much if no one wants to tune in. So Bekker needed to convince consumers in a struggling economy that they should pay for his service (more about this in the next chapter). This was where he needed the financial backing that Vosloo and Nasionale Pers could provide.

Some commentators point to a long-standing culture of venture capitalism in Naspers that presumably played an important role in the decision to invest in pay-TV.

Punts such as the initial launch of *De Burger* and *De Huisgenoot*, the acquisition of *Volksblad*, and the founding of *Fair Lady*, *Rapport* and *Beeld* have been cited as indications of the company's daring and entrepreneurial approach.[37] But those ventures were all in print media – a business it was comfortable in. Sure, every new publication had its perils, but embarking on such a venture was not completely foreign to Nasionale Pers. M-Net was something different. It was a shot in the dark – but one that Vosloo was willing to fire.

In the Afrikaner establishment of the early 1980s, Vosloo could, just like Bekker, be classified as *verlig* (enlightened). He was open to the idea of talks with banned political movements such as the African National Congress (ANC), and realised that apartheid's stringent social engineering could not last forever. Vosloo's assertion in a *Beeld* editorial in 1981 that the country would have a black president one day provoked a furore in NP circles. Still, on the broader political spectrum – from left to right – he ranked as a conservative. He had the ear of those in power for the very reason that he was seen as not too radical.

So Nasionale Pers might not have been run by the most conservative of conservatives, but it was certainly conservatively run. Notoriously stingy with dividend payments, the company had plenty of funds in reserve. A clear indication of the mindset: Piet Cillié, board chairman in the 1980s, and former editor of *Die Burger*, avoided talking about 'profits', preferring to use the term 'surplus' instead.[38] This evoked the image of a public service institution rather than a company operating with the goal of rewarding shareholders.

Veteran investor Mof Terreblanche underlined this financial conservatism in a 2007 tribute to Vosloo. 'Nasionale Pers was the only company to my knowledge to which the auditors attached a positive qualification every year – in other words, the auditors reckoned the company ascribed too low a value to its assets,' he wrote.[39]

As a result, cash-flow problems or solvency concerns were not a feature of the Nasionale Pers books. In 1985, the company reported a total debt to equity ratio of 0,58:1. And despite complaining about dwindling advertising revenue, it chalked up a profit of nearly R11 million.[40]

Financially, the company was able to invest in a venture such as M-Net. Vosloo then had the political savvy to get the government's blessing and to string together an alliance of divergent, and at times belligerent, press groups to supply the rest of the funding.

Now, the MBA graduate had to prove he could build a business. Bekker had to convince people he could do magic.

3.

CONVINCE OTHERS YOU DO MAGIC

'When I was young, the word *entrepreneur* was still French. You know, it wasn't used.' — KOOS BEKKER, 2014[1]

'The moment of gestation is a sacred moment. There is something magical in creation.' — KOOS BEKKER, 2015[2]

H ALLEY'S COMET SHAVED PAST OUR PLANET IN 1986. THIS HAPPENS once, maybe twice, in a lifetime. Unfortunately, this celestial object was not as visible as it had been during earlier cycles, and many would-be viewers were disappointed.

In that year, Koos Bekker also set out to get viewers hooked on something he was about to send through the sky. And he was aiming for a fat tail.

'We calculated a break-even subscriber number. And we did not know this at the time, but Koos asked for a package to incentivise this break-even point, rather than earning a fixed salary,' Chris von Ulmenstein, who had been seconded to M-Net from the advertising agency Young & Rubicam (Y&R), wrote in her memoir, *SwitchBitch*.[3]

Setting up a subscription television business would need proper marketing, and Bekker appointed Y&R to put M-Net on the map. In the late

1970s, Bekker himself had done a stint in advertising at a Cape Town-based advertising agency, McKinstry Schönfeldt.[4]

His bosses held him in such high regard that they helped pay for his MBA in the United States, Von Ulmenstein recounted. By the time Bekker returned to South Africa, his old agency had been absorbed by Y&R, which is why he offered them the account.

Together with Y&R, Bekker set out to determine what would attract subscribers to M-Net – or, more accurately, what irritated them about the SABC. Viewers' biggest gripe was the constant advertising interruptions during programmes, Von Ulmenstein writes.

In the US, HBO initially caught the attention of consumers by positioning itself as a provider of movies without ad breaks. Paired with quality sports content, it was enough to put the American pay-TV business on the map.[5]

This would be Bekker's strategy in South Africa too. Lots of movies, and no ads while they were running. To round it off, Bekker's flicks would be much fresher. M-Net's licence allowed it to broadcast films eighteen months after their box office releases, while the SABC had to wait for no less than eight years.

By the time *Back to the Future* could air on TV1, for example, M-Net would have screened the movie and both its sequels a long time before. By then, the original would probably be at the bottom of a video store's bargain bin.

'The SABC had gone stale. This was the gap Koos saw,' says Andrew Halley-Wright, another Y&R planning head who worked on the M-Net account in the early years.[6]

It's strange to imagine in the 2020s, but back then the SABC still dubbed foreign TV series into Afrikaans, with the original audio broadcast simultaneously over a radio channel. It was such a phenomenon in South Africa that TV sets were sold with a built-in 'simulcast' function – for those viewers who preferred to hear Pierce Brosnan's voice instead of Pierre Bosman's in *Remington Steele*.

Censorship was also a real buzzkiller. Some films were banned out-right, and the state broadcaster itself curated its content, tilting it towards the 'wholesome family entertainment' side.

When selecting the programmes, the SABC often applied 'stricter morals' than the Publication Board, the broadcaster's director-general, Riaan (Koedoe) Eksteen, remarked in 1986.[7] Expletives and profanity were a no-no. Suggesting sex was okay, but showing it was certainly not.

Bekker and his young team latched on to the opportunity to cast the office bearers at the state broadcaster as ageing white males who had spent their lives working in a bureaucracy. They wanted to capitalise on the public perception of the SABC's institutional conservatism.

When Eksteen chastised M-Net for listing *Soap*, a satire of overly sexy soap operas, on its first programming schedules, Bekker retorted that it was much tamer than *Dallas*, which the SABC had been airing for years. 'Only someone with no sense of humour can misunderstand it the way Mr Eksteen does,' sniped Bekker.[8]

But it would be wrong to paint Eksteen as an obstacle to progress. Having made his name as a South African representative at the United Nations in the late 1970s, he actually tried to find a diplomatic solution to the looming battle between the SABC and M-Net.

In 1985, he used the state broadcaster's new entertainment channel – TV4 – to broker a lucrative deal with Ton Vosloo as chair of the pay-TV consortium. The SABC would take a 30 per cent stake in M-Net in ex-change for 30 per cent of TV4.[9] What a bargain!

With an operating agreement, Vosloo could smooth the road for the launch of the subscription television service, as the SABC's infrastructure would help the new channel sign up more subscribers in a wider area. For Eksteen, it had the benefit that the state broadcaster would not be em-broiled in expensive bidding wars for sporting events.

Unfortunately – and especially so for the taxpayer – SABC chair Dr Brand Fourie later torpedoed the deal, claiming that M-Net would never be viable.[10] Swopping 30 per cent of one channel for 30 per cent of what would later become a multibillion-rand enterprise just did not make sense at the time. So M-Net had to go it alone.

But before the channel could even start with regular programming, it had to make sure enough people would watch. Bekker wanted viewers to tune their sets so as to make M-Net one of their regular channels. And they wouldn't even need a decoder to do so. For that purpose, he and Vosloo had negotiated an important concession as part of the broadcasting licence: an 'open' slot of an hour or two a day in which they could reach viewers who did not have decoders. It would be a useful marketing tool to showcase content free of charge, enticing would-be subscribers to take the plunge and buy a decoder.

When it came to the first test transmission, it was Cobus Stofberg who saw an opportunity. M-Net's first broadcast would be a rugby game on a Saturday – nothing less than the 1986 Currie Cup final between Transvaal and Western Province.

Luckily for them, a maverick was running rugby at Johannesburg's Ellis Park Stadium – none other than the fertiliser tycoon Louis Luyt. 'Louis had a fight with the SABC and the Rugby Board, so he said, "you guys come in to Ellis Park and you broadcast",' recalls Vosloo.[11]

With South African teams still banned from international sport, the Currie Cup final was as big as it got. 'What made the idea attractive was that it was high profile. People wouldn't go to that effort for a kiddies' programme,' Bekker told an interviewer a few days after this historic transmission early in September 1986.[12]

In setting up M-Net, he ran a tight ship. Most of the project was ahead of schedule and below budget, so less than a fortnight after the broadcasting equipment had been installed and tested, the Randburg centre was ready to go.

Bekker was sceptical, though. 'I said, we couldn't take such a risk. But the technical people kept on saying we could do it. By Tuesday evening we had decided to go for it. Since then, no one here has slept. We worked day and night to get the thing on the air,' he added.[13]

The move even made a bit of a media splash ahead of the scheduled broadcasts that were due to start the next month. The game was won by Western Province, which retained the Currie Cup in what would be the last of its hallowed '*vyf goue jare*' (five golden years). It would be a while before M-Net struck gold.

With a decoder, and after paying a monthly subscription, you had access to all that M-Net had to offer. Without it, you could watch only a few programmes for free during the daily slot that soon became known as Open Time. Seven in the evening was the threshold when the 'haves' kept enjoying exclusive content, but the 'have-nots' were left staring at a scrambled screen.

'You haven't got it until you get it,' was the phrase M-Net settled on to drive home the idea of insiders versus outsiders. And the team at Y&R then pulled together footage from the movies the channel was about to premiere, creating a montage that would make any film lover salivate, recalls Halley-Wright.[14]

They later paired this with M-Net's version of a Queen song. 'Don't stop me now' became 'We won't stop now' as the new channel wanted to be known for non-stop entertainment (and, later, uninterrupted 'magic').

Bekker and his team started by installing 500 decoders. They were cautious, because no pay-TV station in the United States or Europe had managed to launch its services without some kind of technical disaster. In France, for example, one out of ten decoders distributed by Canal+ had failed.

'We're taking things slowly; testing a few at a time and progressing systematically,' Bekker told the *Financial Mail* in October. Initially, the only hiccup was the screening of M-Net's very first commercial as sixty seconds of darkness, when a technician forgot to connect a plug.[15]

M-Net had a limited number of decoders. So the first ones were aimed at multiple users who lived in blocks of flats. Unfortunately for Bekker and his team, those multi-unit devices could only be installed if a majority of occupants approved, and were willing to pay the monthly subscriptions.

Part of M-Net's allure was its keeping-up-with-the-Joneses factor. Or even getting ahead of those snooty Joneses. But this factor was neutralised in a block of flats where a board of trustees made decisions on behalf of all the owners. Not only was access often denied, but because old Jones next door watched the same SABC channels as you, envy could not go viral in the way a good marketer would want it to.

Hotels were another major target, but the country's economic woes and increasing isolation dampened both leisure and business travel.

On top of that, the SABC rejigged its programming schedule as soon as M-Net went live, using TV4 to take the battle for viewership to the new channel, especially in Open Time. Apart from being an important marketing tool for the pay channel, the window also became a valuable source of advertising revenue. Facing the SABC head-on was not ideal.

The first phase, directed at hotels and apartments, was a disaster, and by March 1987 the business was floundering, with losses accumulating at R3,5 million a month, Bekker recalled years later.[16] The pay-TV start-up had to tap its investors for more funds. Most of the press groups grudgingly obliged, but Perskor pulled out. M-Net also had to rack up debt to stay in the game.[17]

By this stage, well over R100 million had been piled into the venture, says finance chief Steve Pacak.[18] The new business was against the ropes. But back in 1975, pay-TV icon HBO had actually used a bout between Muhammad Ali and Joe Frazier to make its mark. The 'Thrilla in Manila' had been a game changer for HBO. So M-Net tried something similar.

'The big cut-through, I think, came when I packaged the Hagler-Leonard fight,' remembers marketing head Chris Raats.[19] For the world middleweight title, Sugar Ray Leonard beat Marvin Hagler on points, but it was M-Net that scored a knockout with its early morning live broadcast from Las Vegas. Decoders sold out nationwide, and subscriber numbers climbed to 90 000.[20]

The fight coincided with the roll-out of the first decoders for single homes. 'Suddenly the market took off,' said Bekker.

In the latter half of the tumultuous 1980s, while the politics were ugly and the future uncertain, a number of things started working in M-Net's favour. Pay-TV's carefree entertainment could be positioned as a welcome escape from the riots, extrajudicial killings and general instability that marked the death throes of apartheid.

Halley-Wright remembers how, when putting M-Net's first advertising campaigns together, they drew inspiration from the best-seller *The Popcorn Report*. In this book, the futurist Faith Popcorn first coined the term 'cocooning', defined as 'the impulse to stay inside when the outside gets too tough and scary'. In the United States, this meant pressures of work and keeping up with the neighbours.

'But in South Africa, the crime and violence now beginning to really rage meant that most of us privileged ones "cocooned", scared shitless, behind high walls, alarm systems and watchdogs,' Halley-Wright recounts.[21] Public spaces increasingly became places of conflict.

Even positive developments caused disruptions. By the mid-1980s, South Africans spent some R150 million a year at the box office. But when movie theatres were opened to all in 1987, a number of cinemas did not immediately embrace this change. The authorities then forced the theatres that were still discriminating along racial lines to cease all screenings. This was but one of a host of problems facing businesses in South Africa's entertainment industry.[22]

A gaping hole had opened in the social lives of hundreds of thousands of people, and a fortune in recreational spending was up for grabs. Cleverly, M-Net filled the void.

After starting with broadcasts in Johannesburg and Pretoria, the service was expanded to Durban and Pietermaritzburg in August 1987, and to Cape Town two months later.

The decoder became an aspirational product. As M-Net's popularity grew, more and more consumers considered forking out R595 for a decoder and paying the subscription of R29 a month. At that time, a litre of petrol sold for about 50 cents, so a month of home entertainment cost the same as a tank of fuel.

For M-Net, breaking even meant selling about 150 000 decoders nation-wide, a target Bekker was aiming to achieve by February 1988.[23] To accelerate adoption, the company drew on a R30 million facility from TrustBank to finance hire purchase agreements for potential subscribers.[24] It also borrowed R30 million from Volkskas.[25]

The team puzzled out how best to market these devices. They soon realised movies were a decent motivator, but that sport was the real clincher when it came to convincing the head of a household to invest in a decoder.

Thanks to the exclusive broadcast of a few strategic sporting events in 1987 – those boxing title bouts, English soccer derbies and European test rugby – tens of thousands of breadwinners were willing to sign on.

'In the early days of M-Net, the company went through such a fast growth curve that we often found ourselves caught with our pants down. I can recall several weekends during which the team of top managers packed decoders for shipping or answered calls in the customer service centre,' Stofberg remembers.[26]

Some fairly recent advances in consumer electronics also aided the company's rapid expansion. Though TV on demand was still decades away, taping a programme on a video cassette recorder (VCR) was a good alternative.

'Initially, we thought we'd be competing with VCRs, but now we've found that the complementary aspect is stronger than the competitive,' Bekker observed a few months after M-Net's first broadcast. 'If we can hook just one in two of South Africa's 600 000 VCR owners, we'll have achieved our objective.'[27]

By the mid-1980s, economic sanctions and the weaker rand had sharply pushed up the price of television sets. Fortunately for Bekker, 1987 was an election year; politicians promised to stimulate the local electronics industry, and changes in excise duties lowered the cost of television sets by nearly a quarter. This made TV sets a few hundred rands cheaper, a useful nudge towards affording one of M-Net's Delta 9000 decoders.

Before Christmas 1988, M-Net had sold more than 200 000 decoders.[28] All of these subscribers were paying a monthly fee. Clearly, they were happy to sign on, and as their numbers rose, investors also started smiling.

Broadcasting services such as the SABC initially attract a lot of attention and lure in a large number of viewers, Bekker told an interviewer in 1986. 'A year later, those viewer numbers are more or less the same, and the same goes for your cash flow.'[29]

With pay-TV, however, the selling is done more gradually, almost from door to door. Only those who can afford the service signs up. It takes time to gain traction. 'In the beginning, your income is small, but your expenses are big. Over time, however, there is great potential because your expenses remain almost constant,' Bekker explained.[30]

Even though subscription income represented more than three-quarters of the company's revenue, advertising was a useful contributor. And advertisers had much greater certainty about whom they could reach on the channel. In the meantime, television's share of total advertising was still rising, advancing to 30 per cent in 1988 from 28 per cent two years earlier.[31]

What made M-Net's growth so extraordinary is that it came at a time when just about everything else was struggling. M-Net was not only pocketing recurring income, but also growing its subscriber base. 'Initially you run at a loss, but when you start making a profit, you make an ever larger profit,' Bekker added.[32]

By 1990, the company was making a profit of R20 million and forecasting earnings of more than R30 million for the following year.[33] Bekker was eyeing much more.

And so, M-Net announced its plans to list on the JSE, mainly to enhance its capital base and to facilitate expansion, both through organic growth and acquisitions. In its prospectus, the company referred to its own success as one of the first two pay-TV services outside the United States, and hinted that there were promising prospects in other countries.

Great excitement surrounded the listing plans, not least because M-Net subscribers were also offered the opportunity to subscribe for shares.

Hoping to raise R20 million in its stock market debut, the company offered 15 million shares of R1 each to its 430 000 subscribers, and another 5 million to selected individuals and institutions.[34]

M-Net started trading at R1,20 per share. In its first twelve months the stock soared by 322 per cent, making it the JSE's best performer of the year. The listing made it clear that the bulk of the press groups' value now lay in the stakes they held in the pay-TV business. They were clever to make that initial investment, and were now reaping the rewards.

Bekker, Stofberg and other employees also got the chance to get their hands on the stock. Nearly 10 per cent of the company's issued share capital was kept in an employee incentive trust and offered to participating members at the price on the date of listing, but redeemable at any time within ten years. A few millionaires were made.

In the meantime, M-Net kept gaining subscribers. Late in 1991, Bekker and his team launched a new decoder: the Compact 9000. A cheaper alternative to the Delta 9000, it was a clever push to get into many more homes by the time the first ball of the 1992 Cricket World Cup was bowled.

M-Net had the exclusive rights to broadcast the event. From the upset victory in their opening game against defending champions Australia, the Proteas' progress was keenly followed from South Africa. Some 40 000 new M-Net subscribers signed on in February and March, most of them to watch the tournament.[35]

The extra sales lifted South Africa to one of the highest pay-TV penetration rates in the world, as one in four households with a colour television set also owned a decoder.[36] It also cemented Bekker's reputation as a global trailblazer in the TV industry.

With the Compact 9000 nearly 40 per cent cheaper than the Delta 9000, he was also expanding his market to less affluent consumers.

Yet another decoder followed: the Delta 9000 Plus. Released a few months after the tournament, this was aimed at attracting viewers with other needs. It could connect to a personal computer and pick up both M-Net and SABC's TV1 outside its usual transmission areas if plugged into a satellite dish and receiver.

The company had already started a satellite broadcasting service the previous year to reach second-tier cities such as Nelspruit (now Mbombela), Pietersburg (now Polokwane) and Richards Bay.

This system enabled M-Net to look further afield, as subscribers in other African countries could be served via satellite. In 1992, M-Net International was launched, a channel stripped of the content specific to South Africa, and aimed at other parts of the continent.

Armed with the new decoder, Bekker was eyeing not only TV-starved affluent consumers who lived out in the sticks, but also business clients. Some wanted news feeds or data services. This is why M-Net acquired Information Trust Corporation (ITC), a company with data on more than half a million businesses, and credit information on 7 million individuals.

Though the public perceived M-Net as a 'showbiz station', Bekker saw entertainment as a means to do business, even if this did not sound terribly exciting. And he was keen to use his infrastructure – all the broadcasting equipment, the know-how, and more than half a million decoders in South African homes – to beam data to those who could use it and pay for it.

'M-Net's communications technologies division is now using conventional broadcast signals to convey data over the air from computer to computer,' he announced in 1992.[37]

Supplying services to other businesses made sense, even if this turned out to be the state broadcaster. M-Net's subscriber management division developed a strategy to market the company's satellite service in the rest of Africa. It started with the satellite subscribers of its old rival, the SABC, and the BBC's World Service Television outside South Africa.

Around the same time, Bekker and M-Net started looking for new markets across the border. It started with Lesotho, but Namibia, Swaziland and Botswana were also in its sights.[38]

M-Net's deeper African safari began in 1991 when it acquired a stake in an independent Kenyan TV station. Besides holding 50 per cent of the company's shares, M-Net would also provide decoders and subscription services.[39]

As broadcasting is a political game, Bekker had to find a way to wriggle into markets without having to do all the time-consuming smooching up front. He used the technology his company had acquired and developed as well as his team's industry experience to gain access to new territories.

Kenya is a good example of this approach, but he also took M-Net's tech and know-how to more 'developed' markets, where pay-TV operators were still finding their feet.

By late 1991, M-Net had raised more than R254 million in a rights issue and struck a deal with tobacco and luxury goods tycoon Johann Rupert. They would use the cash Rupert's Richemont group had offshore to acquire a Dutch business named FilmNet. Though it was the largest pay-TV outfit in northern Europe, with operations in six countries, it still had fewer subscribers than M-Net.

For a few years, Bekker and his team worked to grow subscriber numbers and expand to other countries. But he did not see FilmNet as a provider of pay-TV channels only – he wanted it to provide subscription management services to other companies that lacked the technology or resources to bill their clients efficiently in different countries.[40]

He was happy to compete in one field, but to make money off those same competitors in another. That's why, in 1994, Bekker and his team separated MultiChoice, which at the time handled subscriptions, from the FilmNet channel. He wanted to supply other channels with services. He also concluded a further deal with Rupert, piling the FilmNet assets into a new entity called NetHold (more about this in chapter 14).

'We'll be very much a platform for other people's channels. We'll put together a cluster (of TV channels) for them, price it and split the reve-nue,' he announced in 1995.[41]

That same year, he concluded a $500 million deal with electronics manufacturers Philips, National Panasonic and Pace Micro Technology.

'Someone needed to take the risk and put down the serious money,' said Bekker after a transaction which saw NetHold buying 1.1 million digital decoders.[42] The shift from analogue to digital was coming, and Bekker wanted to be in the forefront.

'The next step is the leap to digital. The start of digital television will be by far the biggest change since the introduction of colour,' he declared.[43]

At home, he also pushed the switchover to digital. It carried the promise of a multitude of channels that would enable the business to target programming at specific market segments.

'Koos was way ahead of anyone else on this thing. He could see the future lay in digital – not just for clearer pictures, but to go multichannel and get the economies of scale in a satellite footprint. It was enormously expensive – quite mind-boggling – and a lot of people balked at the sheer enormity of it,' says long-time M-Net executive and later MultiChoice CEO Nolo Letele.[44]

At the time, Vosloo writes, MultiChoice had been upgrading its analogue system, and Bekker's digital plan caught the technical team off guard, adding: 'This leap was typical of Koos. He has an instinctive feel for promising innovations.'[45]

In this digital era, Bekker positioned his group as a provider of pay-TV technology to the rest of the world. In 1995, he claimed exporting decoders was the most successful consumer electronics product in South Africa's history, with orders and shipments totalling more than R200 million that year.[46]

He had also been investing heavily to develop more digital tech through the Dutch company Irdeto, which by this time was an MIH subsidiary, finding clients in Canada, Australia and Thailand.

Strangely, when M-Net started to expand into the rest of Africa, governments were worried that it might spew nationalist rhetoric. Letele, who did some footwork on the continent, was sometimes accompanied by Bekker to places such as Namibia, Zimbabwe, Kenya, Zambia, Ghana and Nigeria. At home, apartheid was still government policy.

'It was quite a challenge. I had to stress that we were an entertainment channel and did not carry news, so we weren't going to export any propaganda,' Letele recounts.[47]

Between Bekker, Letele and the rest of the team they convinced the gatekeepers and by the mid-1990s, their business had subscribers in thirty-one countries on the continent.

Hard to imagine that by the mid-1980s, Naspers was still a single-country business. A decade later, through M-Net and MultiChoice, it would have a line in the water in more than forty.

These opportunities were all thanks to Bekker's image as a wealth creator. Colleagues, clients and investors believed he could do magic – a phrase echoing the M-Net theme song and advertising slogan, 'We Won't Stop the Magic'. Vosloo not only says 'the man is brilliant', but also calls him 'the talisman'.

Bekker's reputation would eventually see him at the helm of the business that first backed him, where – as CEO – he could reshape that company.

4.

RESHAPE YOUR COMPANY

'You can buy the whole of the New York Times today for
$2,5 billion. We can buy it. We're not interested.'

– KOOS BEKKER, 2008[1]

'Newspapers are history.'

– KOOS BEKKER, 1990s[2]

KOOS BEKKER TOOK THE REINS OF AN EIGHTY-TWO-YEAR-OLD
company best known for publishing Afrikaans-language newspapers,
books and magazines. He was forty-something, and the job would free
him from constant flying across Europe, the stress of pulling deals together and the homesickness of working abroad. A casual observer might
have thought this would be his *aftree-joppie* (retirement job). Think again.

Though he would remain in that same CEO job until retirement,
Bekker was far from kicking back. The electronic media entrepreneur
was only getting started. Over the next few years he would mould
a traditional print media group into what could best be described as
a Sun City slot machine – an apparatus for winning big. Some, perhaps
kinder, commentators would call it a venture capital business or a tech
investment company.

Originally, in 1915, the company was certainly not set up to use other people's money to chase the jackpot. The founders of Nasionale Pers were idealists, even ideologues. They wanted to use their single product, a Cape Town-based Afrikaans-language newspaper, as the starting point to agitate, educate and motivate.

As its first editor, *De Burger* had Dr Daniel François Malan, a *dominee* (minister) who preached in Graaff-Reinet. 'Our salvation lies in the awakening of our feeling of national unity. *De Burger* will guide and strengthen this feeling,' Malan wrote in his first editorial.

His definition of national unity was, of course, quite narrow. With this newspaper, Nasionale Pers aimed to bind Afrikaners together, to uplift what they perceived to be a downtrodden *volk*.

Three decades later, and with the support of Nasionale Pers, Malan led the NP to an election victory, wooing a majority of white voters with his policy of apartheid. Tragically, uplifting the downtrodden Afrikaner would entail some heavy treading on others.

When Bekker walked in as the new boss, he must have encountered some of that idealism. Solidarity with the cause of Afrikaners – broadened, in the new South Africa, to Afrikaans speakers – would have pulsed through the veins of many a senior staffer. Less than a decade earlier, his predecessor, Ton Vosloo, had still called the company a *'volkstrust'* (people's trust).

Also, Bekker arrived only weeks after the company, with Vosloo at the helm, had snubbed the Truth and Reconciliation Commission (TRC), the body set up to examine human rights abuses during the apartheid era and grant amnesty to those perpetrators who had 'come clean' about their actions, thereby promoting national reconciliation. Chaired by Archbishop Desmond Tutu, it began its hearings in the mid-1990s.

In 1997, the Commission requested a submission from Nasionale Pers about the media's role in the period from 1960 to 1994. Not an unreasonable request, seeing that the company had openly supported the NP or, as Bekker later put it, 'fully participated in apartheid'.[3]

Vosloo replied that the company's role in the history of the country was available in *Oor Grense Heen*, a publication marking the first three-quarters of a century of its existence.[4] Neither Vosloo, members of his senior management, or long-time editors of prominent Nasionale Pers publications made an appearance at the TRC.

However, some Nasionale Pers journalists, led by *Beeld* deputy editor Tim du Plessis, did make a submission to the Commission. Together, they stated that the company's newspapers had formed an integral part of the power structure that had implemented and maintained apartheid.[5] Citing the publications' role in supporting the NP in elections and referendums, for instance, they declared that although they had not personally perpetrated any human rights abuses, they felt morally responsible. The statement was endorsed by 127 of the company's journalists.[6]

This happened in Vosloo's last week as chief executive, and stoked controversy within the press group and outside it. The old guard was unhappy about what it saw as disloyalty from junior staff. Juniors, in turn, felt that history was being made by breaking with the past, and who were the old geezers to stand in their way? Later that year, Bekker remarked that it was an 'unhappy saga which hurt many people and which hopefully was now at an end'.[7] In its final report, the Commission lamented the company's refusal to participate.

Vosloo, of course, played his own role in South Africa's transition from minority rule to democracy. First as newspaper editor and later as media boss, he had the ear of many government figures, and claims to have steered public opinion in a conciliatory direction.

But his greatest feat was to use the political uncertainty as motivation for listing Nasionale Pers publicly on the JSE. Until then, it was a privately held company with only 2 860 shareholders. This move, in 1994, would be a vital step in leaving the idea of a public service institution behind, and turning the company into a 'normal', commercially oriented corporation.

'Unfortunately, the way we handle our shares – the limits to voting rights and trading – creates the impression that we are unwaveringly clinging to control, to the extent that we are a "*volkstrust*",' Vosloo stated in a document presented to the Nasionale Pers board in January that year.[8]

Suddenly, being a *volkstrust* was a bad thing. Having fewer than 3 000 shareholders and no discernible entity or group in control was not good either.

Vosloo reckoned it made the company vulnerable to a new government that might not be as friendly as their old pals in the NP. 'At the moment we are a "soft target", judging by the increasingly bad publicity we are getting for our supposed favouring flowing from improper relations with the government,' he added.[9]

Despite pulling other press groups with daily papers into the pay-TV venture, those which only had weeklies or magazines were smarting from being left out, and some publications were poking at Vosloo's company with editorial pens dipped in poisoned ink. High-flying M-Net was the reason there was money in the bank, and substantial value in Nasionale Pers's privately held shares.

This was why Vosloo wanted the listing – to get the broader public on Nasionale Pers's side. And so, on 12 September 1994, the company made its debut on the JSE.

Pure altruism? Getting the new nation to accept the company in a new guise? Sure, but the move also made many insiders rich. Vosloo later boasted that the listing had instantly created 1 200 millionaires.[10]

Among those, of course, was Vosloo himself. As executive chair, he was in an ideal position to benefit. In the year Nasionale Pers was listed, directors held some 1,7 per cent of shares. On its first day on the bourse, the stock rallied from its last tender price of R7 to R21, scaling a market cap of R2,3 billion. The board members' stake was worth some R40 million on day one.

Since 1987, senior management had also been awarded stock in the company to incentive performance. So more than a few executives smoked big cigars on the day Nasionale Pers listed.

Though not in Bekker's league, by the time Vosloo retired as chair in 2014, he had also made a few hundred million rands. So it's fair to say that Naspers's listing had not been for the sake of the broader interests of the *volk* alone.

It was the start of a decoupling from the company's founding rationale; it would create wealth, but also unhappiness among those who believed Nasionale Pers still had a deeper calling.

Veteran stockbroker and investor Mof Terreblanche had done a presentation to the board about the pros and cons of listing. 'Some directors were of the view that a listing would eventually lead to the loss of the company's independence, and specifically that it would lose its "Afrikaans culture",' he recalled in 2007.[11]

The listing was not the only signal to government and the broader community that the company, from a new South Africa perspective, was going legit. Within a year, the Nasionale Pers board sported two directors of colour.

More importantly, the move enabled Bekker to soup the business up later for riskier ventures. If you get paid like an entrepreneur, you want your company to win big. Vosloo had started the reshaping. Bekker would take it further.

In 1997, newspapers and magazines accounted for 32 per cent of the group's revenue, which shows that Nasionale Pers was already steadily moving away from print. M-Net's contribution was the driving force behind this change as television platforms contributed R2,4 billion, or 56 per cent.

Though revenue can provide clues about where a business is going, profit tells you where the money is being made. Together, magazines and newspapers contributed nearly R193 million to operating income, whereas the other segments racked up losses of R183 million.

'We in the publishing world are ready for the ride of our lives,' reads a joint statement by Bekker and board chair Vosloo later that year.[12]

Setting out a vision for the future, the two declared that Naspers was no longer an orthodox printing and publishing house, but that products on paper were still its backbone and would remain so for a long time to come. 'In fact, for ever, if we are reading the signs right,' the statement proclaimed.[13] Now that's a line that hasn't aged well. In print forever?

One that looks a bit better a quarter of a century later is: 'Take the content you have at your disposal, and aim it at the market you want to exploit by using the relevant technology.'[14]

And so, Bekker (presumably) talked about interactive television and the shopping and banking opportunities it promised to bring to every lounge chair in the world.

Naspers, as the company would soon be renamed, was going to push deeper into TV, and was hoping to marry this with some of its existing content. The advent of the internet (then still written with a capital I) was set to be the force that created enormous opportunities for the publisher, they added.

And create opportunities it did. But not in the way they might have thought. The World Wide Web was hardly a lucrative new outlet for Naspers's existing content: too many news outlets started by posting their stories for free, and that killed the market for paying subscribers.

The real opportunities lay in the software entrepreneurs refining the technology and making it usable for the masses. It became a hotbed of investment activity – a place where any business with cash could take a punt and possibly make billions (more in chapter 6).

What Naspers had was an enterprise with a useful combination in its stable. Print media may not be the most exciting business to be in when it comes to growth or profitability, but it does give its owner a steady cash flow.

Establishing a title such as a newspaper or a magazine is costly. *Beeld*, for example, ran at a loss for most of its first decade. But after many years of vertical integration, such as investing in its own printing capacity, Naspers had more control than some of its rivals over the input costs facing its titles.

Even with newspaper circulation and advertising revenue declining year after year, it simply would not fall to zero overnight, which gave management the opportunity to implement cost-cutting measures, and keep the cash flowing.

Some of the cash from those operations could then be deployed in other fields with more growth potential – similar to the funding provided to M-Net in the 1980s.

While print media and publishing were 'legacy assets' dating from the company's earliest days, Bekker also got custody of the so-called M-group of businesses. This included a 26,5 per cent stake in M-Net. As a business he had built himself, he had a good idea of its potential.

In 1997, this pay-TV venture made a profit of nearly R54 million. But it was still launching new channels and pushing deeper into the South African market and the rest of Africa. The next year, it reported a loss of R96 million.

M-Net, through M-Cell, also held a 29 per cent stake in the cellular provider MTN, which at that stage was still making losses, but seemed to have potential.

Another company that starts with an M is MIH. The substantial profits realised from its investment in and then disposal of NetHold and FilmNet provided Bekker with some manoeuvring room for the transactions he was probably already planning as he moved into the CEO's office.

Naspers was not Bekker's first reshaping of a long-established enterprise. In the 1970s, as editor of *Die Matie*, he managed to bring the per page cost of Stellenbosch's student rag down despite a rise in the prices of paper and printing.[15]

Bekker beefed up distribution and intensified advertising sales, more than doubling the revenue from that source. He introduced a special first-years' edition, which earned a healthy sum in advertising. In another edition, he trialed full-colour printing which was available thanks to the shift in technology from hot lead to phototype.

'An axiom of our trade is that content is king,' Bekker said in 2010, echoing his days as a student journalist. 'This is true only if technology stays constant. As soon as that moves to the next level, you'd better lift yourself fast, since no content in the world will save the bacon of a tech laggard.'[16]

But that was at a single student paper. Naspers had a whole stable of print media assets, and was the biggest publisher in the country.

An important part of Bekker's reshaping had actually started long before he joined the upper echelon of the company. Back at M-Net, he had assembled a young team and bedded down an informal culture. 'You know, when we started, we attracted the cowboys – people who were prone to taking risks,' Bekker recalled later.[17]

Several of his senior colleagues at M-Net would bubble through to the company where he now had the top job. M-Net's finance chief, Steve Pacak, soon became CFO at Naspers. And Cobus Stofberg, who was already running MIH, joined the Naspers board.

Bekker also repositioned some other key people who had been recruited through M-Net. One of them was Hans Hawinkels, who joined the pay-TV business to further its expansion into Africa. Hawinkels, who had cut his teeth at Sol Kerzner's entertainment group Satbel, was earmarked by Bekker to seek investment opportunities in the Far East.

With a new team at the top, some of whom he had worked with for more than a decade, he could go about executing his strategy. Then came the pivot.

It could be summarised as follows: the internet was king, and the Far East was the next big thing. Everything else, with a few exceptions, had to either generate cash to fund this, or get out of the way.

At a meeting of the company's highest office bearers, the new CEO called newspapers and magazines 'information pounded into tree trunks,' remembers Du Plessis, then editor of *Rapport*.[18] Not the sort of comment that would endear you to a room full of managers who had built their careers in print journalism. But it showed Bekker's resolve.

In his first year on the job, Naspers started the internet service provider (ISP) M-Web. Bekker wanted to make web browsing as easy as turning on the television or radio. Unlike TV, the phenomenon was not only a recent addition in South Africa, it was new to the world. This was long before apps or social media sites, and even e-commerce was still in its infancy.

To think that all the excitement was for something as tardy as dial-up internet – whirring modems and speeds of barely 56 kilobits per second. And where to go once you're on the internet? No Google, no YouTube, no Wikipedia, and most local businesses did not have websites. Nevertheless, after six months M-Web had 35 000 subscribers, and a year later it had 145 000.

Buzz phrases such as the 'global village', 'cyberspace' and the 'information superhighway' were bandied about nearly as much as 'eat my shorts' and 'whatever'. Before the dreaded turn of the century – remember Y2K! – M-Web launched its Big Black Box, an attractively packaged dial-up modem. An ISP was the sort of business that looked familiar to Bekker and his team: signing up subscribers by marketing an aspirational service to them. But this was a cash-guzzling venture, and in 1998 Naspers listed M-Web on the JSE to raise more capital.

Online retailer Kalahari.net (later Kalahari.com) was established that same year, and soon proved a popular shopping destination for books, music and videos. News24 was launched the next year, as part of a broader push into internet publishing through an entity called 24.com.

Naspers also started versions of M-Web in Thailand, Indonesia and China. Though these businesses struggled, the move dipped a toe in lucrative waters, enabling Bekker's man in the Far East to find the deal of the century in Tencent (more in chapter 6).

Earlier that decade, bolstered by the cash flow from its pay-TV business, Naspers had supported M-Net's foray into telecommunications (more in chapter 14). But with MTN still in need of development funding of its own, Bekker now had a difficult decision to make. Actually not that difficult, as he would have fallen well short of the cellular provider's financing needs of more than R5 billion.

Naspers let go of its MTN shares in exchange for a larger stake in M-Web and MIH. Ultimately, it was a choice between cellular telephony and pay-TV. Financing MTN's expansion would have meant slowing the push into pay-TV in places such as Greece, Thailand or the rest of Africa, or even selling some of those assets.

'Bekker recommended that we stick to the television side as cell phones were, in his view, a "mono-product",' writes Vosloo.[19]

This was the time of feature phones and nothing more. That meant emoticons, not emojis, as smartphones were still the stuff of science fiction movies. At the time, Blackberry developer RIM was tinkering with pagers, and Steve Jobs had just returned to Apple, which was mainly selling desktop computers. Eventually, better mobile phones would change the way people communicate and socialise.

More than a decade later, Bekker lamented that MTN had turned into a great business. '[S]taying in would have been attractive, but we didn't have the bucks to keep both,' he acknowledged.[20]

MTN grew into one of the largest mobile operators in emerging markets, sprawling into the rest of Africa, the Middle East and even South East Asia. By venturing into markets where others feared to tread, it later raked in substantial profits from populous nations such as Nigeria and Iran. But providing the infrastructure is not the most profitable part of the value chain, especially as call volumes declined and text messages all but disappeared, except for inside applications such as WhatsApp.

In recent years, telecommunications companies have tried desperately to be more than just utilities – or a 'dumb pipe' business – supplying data. 'In the case of MTN, we made a ton of money on it. We started MTN initially, but in the end we had to select between the business which has pay-TV, for better or worse, and MTN,' Bekker told an interviewer in 2008.[21]

And letting go of the stake in the mobile operator allowed Bekker to buy out the initial partners in pay-TV.[22] Owning all of its pay-TV assets outright would take a few years to conclude, and M-Net was finally delisted from the JSE in 2004, when changes in accounting standards complicated the company's results.

BEE shareholders in the Phuthuma Futhi scheme, which held 10 per cent of M-Net, were concerned that they would miss out on dividend payments, and requested that Naspers structure a transaction.[23] In a R755 million deal, Naspers acquired the BEE stake and the other 50 per cent of M-Net it did not own at the time.

This followed the reorganisation of MIH in 2002, when the minority interests in MIH Holdings and MIH Limited were swapped for shares in Naspers itself. As a result, MIH Holdings shares were delisted from the JSE, and MIH Limited's shares were delisted from the Nasdaq bourse in the United States. The pay-TV businesses in Greece and Cyprus that Naspers had retained after selling out of NetHold were housed in MIH.

All of these machinations had the result of setting pay-TV up as a cash cow that would support the forays into the internet. And this structure gave Bekker the time to seek out the parts of the internet that made better business sense. Being an ISP, for example, was not the right fit.

Only a decade after establishing M-Web, Naspers sold the business. Though it was very profitable, 'the issue simply is, that we can't run it,' Bekker said in 2009.[24]

Three approaches from potential buyers the previous year had got him thinking about the business. 'We said no, under no condition, no price. Then we relooked at our strategy and we said to ourselves, however much we love the company, it doesn't really fit. We don't have another ISP anywhere in the world. Let's sell it,' he said.[25]

It was part of Bekker's strategy to further reshape Naspers into a media and technology investor instead of sending in troupes of young guns to start new ventures from the ground up.

The most important role of the South African print media business was to be the original cash generator that funded pay-TV's expansion. Bekker did, however, take a punt or two on new initiatives in the newspaper world.

When, after a year of trying to persuade other potential investors, *Daily Sun* founder Deon du Plessis came knocking with the idea of publishing a tabloid for South Africa's largely black working class, Bekker was intrigued. 'He got [the idea] in one. We didn't actually have to explain it. The lights went on,' said Du Plessis in 2005.[26]

The newspaper, notorious for its sexy, hard-to-believe and often folk-lorish content, rapidly grew into the country's biggest daily publication and introduced a new group of newspaper and magazine readers to the medium, claimed Bekker.[27]

Outside South Africa, he made big bets on print media in places such as Brazil and China. But those were investments. Establishing businesses from scratch was not the way Bekker approached his second decade as CEO. It was all about finding the right transaction. And thanks to the cash churning over from print, pay-TV and, increasingly Tencent, he could write the cheques. He could run a venture capital fund without having to be one.

'We looked at some 200 deals last year, and we closed 20. What's very difficult to predict is which deals to do,' he told Moneyweb in 2010.[28] The transactions ranged from big to very big.

The acquisition of Tradus, an eBay-like e-commerce business in Poland, for R15,3 billion in 2008 was an example of the latter. Again, less than a decade later, Naspers nipped and tucked, disposing of Allegro, an on-line retailer it got as part of Tradus. Naspers did not want such a big presence in online retail, not with the likes of Amazon venturing into Eastern Europe.

Over more than a decade and a half as CEO, Bekker shifted the press group to a media company with some interest in ISPs and eventually into a consumer-facing internet business. In the process, he turned Naspers into a truly multinational business.

'We manage the cash flows globally. Internet companies such as Tencent are able quite quickly to pay dividends. It's the pay-TV area that is capital-intensive. The bottom line is that there is cash all over the place. We don't necessarily bring it back to the centre in South Africa. We might use money in China, for instance, to invest in India,' he disclosed in 2011.[29]

An investment in a marketplace such as OLX, followed by more acqui-sitions over time, grew into an entire business segment called online classifieds. Ironically, before the digital era, the classifieds section of news-papers used to be a decent source of cash flow for Naspers. Readers of *Beeld*, *Die Burger* or *Volksblad* were happy to sell anything from second-hand bicycles to personal services through classifieds. Back then, the company provided the platform and pocketed the advertising fees.

But obviously transactions happen much quicker online than in print. And swiping through pictures on a smartphone screen just feels more like shopping than rummaging through printed columns. By the 2020s Naspers, through Prosus, was pocketing more from classifieds than ever before. In 2021, the company estimated the value of online classifieds at $14 billion.

Similarly, Naspers pushed into food delivery. In South Africa it owns Mr D, a humble investment compared with the punts it has taken on Brazil's iFood, India's Swiggy and Delivery Hero in Europe. The move is either brave or stupid, as the company takes the fight to the likes of Uber Eats with a business segment it valued at $18 billion in 2021.

Another, far removed from the print media business Bekker inherited, is online payments. Internet shoppers might be familiar with PayU, which does much of the behind-the-scenes work when a transaction is concluded online. Late in 2021, Naspers placed a value of $11 billion on this business.

And in education technology it owns businesses such as Stack Overflow, Udemy and Codecademy, estimated to be worth more than $5 billion in total by 2021.

As a result, after stepping down and shifting into the role of chairman, Bekker presided over massive movements of capital. With Naspers pushing ever deeper into online classifieds, food delivery, mobile payments and edtech, the company tapped its Tencent treasure trove to drive the strategy home.

A more modest move, in terms of value, happened early in 2019. Naspers's pay-TV assets were unbundled and listed on the JSE as MultiChoice, bringing a thirty-five-year relationship to an end. The business Bekker had started would be part of Naspers no more. His name still adorns an auditorium at the MultiChoice head office in Randburg, Johannesburg, though.

Without registering a blip on its former parent company's share price, MultiChoice created more than R70 billion in shareholder value when it debuted on the JSE.

By the second and third decade of the twenty-first century, Naspers management did not appreciate being called a 'media company' any longer. They preferred 'consumer-facing internet business'. It was the shape in which Bekker had moulded Naspers.

As CEO Bob van Dijk put it shortly after MultiChoice was listed: in 2007 about 90 per cent of the group's revenue was from media – television and print.

'In the heads of many people, we are still a media company, but if you look at where we are today, that has really changed very rapidly. When I took over from Koos [in 2014], the company was about 50-50, media revenue versus consumer internet revenue. And now, after the spinoff of MultiChoice, it's a 100 per cent consumer internet company.'[30]

But what about Media24? The publisher of *Rapport*, *City Press*, *Beeld* and *Die Burger* was still part of Naspers. And it had 'media' in its name!

'If you look at the print part of Media24, it is actually less than half a per cent of our revenue, so if you round it up, it is actually 100 per cent consumer internet,' noted Van Dijk.

And then he pointed out that Media24, like other media companies around the world, was also rapidly transforming into a digital enterprise.[31]

At Naspers, as Bekker remarked decades earlier, newspapers were history.

5.

PITCH AND POSITION LIKE A BOSS

'Koos would pace the floor, shirt hanging out sloppily on the one side, scratching his head and writing down the vision with chalk on the blackboard.'
— ANDREW HALLEY-WRIGHT, 2014[1]

'We won all of our battles because of good preparation.'
— TON VOSLOO, 2018[2]

I N 1973, KOOS BEKKER WAS A FINALIST IN THE DEBATING COM-petition at Stellenbosch University.[3] His knack for public speaking probably came in handy when he campaigned for a spot on the Eendrag house committee later that year.

An election in a university residence is an intimidatingly direct form of democracy. In this case, the 300 or so voters would have known those in the running personally. To get their votes, a candidate needed to be an active participant in res activities, likeable, and also present as some-one who could get the job done – because besides keeping good order, a house committee member managed a portfolio or two.

Bekker had the right mix. He was active on campus as a member of the university's carnival committee and a reporter for *Die Matie*, but also popular enough at home to get elected. He was then tasked with the portfolios of 'Karnaval' social functions and the residence's archive.[4]

Like similar events on other campuses, the annual carnival raised funds for charity. It pitted pairs of residences – one male, one female – against each other in events that included building a float for a procession through town, and raising money with activities such as the sale of *Akkerjol* magazine.

Eendrag joined forces with Heemstede. Small world – this ladies' residence had the same name as the entity with which Naspers would later keep a tight grip on most of its high-voting A-shares. But Bekker was not running a company yet, only a hostel's carnival effort. Nevertheless, it was a daunting job, with many moving parts.

Bekker went all out. To gain publicity he looked into having an airplane fly low over Stellenbosch's town square, Die Braak. To push *Akkerjol* sales he promised a prize for the keenest seller. And he sourced a sponsor of R100 for the float.[5]

'With Mr Koos Bekker heading affairs, Eendrag this year held a particularly successful Karnaval with Heemstede,' reads a report by William Brown, primarius (chair) of the house committee.[6] The effort was characterised by several innovations. For example, it was the first time the float was pulled by four donkeys, he added.

'Karnaval' had subjective aspects, where the winner was decided by a panel of judges, and objective aspects, which hinged on metrics that were easy to measure. Bekker dazzled, but also generated the most cash, and won a trophy as a result.

An early example of his savvy for consumer taste was visible in his other portfolio. As archive boss, he was responsible for Eendrag's newspaper and magazine deliveries. Though Bekker continued with the likes of *Die Burger*, *Time* magazine and *Financial Mail*, he introduced some pin-up magic by adding a subscription to *Scope*.[7]

Add these skills to his later experience in advertising, and it becomes clearer how he was able to hook Ton Vosloo with that phone call a decade later. And how he then convinced Naspers veteran Jan Prins in the Russian Tea Room in New York to recommend to Vosloo that the MBA graduate be brought from Columbia to South Africa to make a case for pay-TV.

Then, of course, the slide projector jammed and had to be restarted with a pair of scissors. But as Prins remembered: 'Bekker's presentation was excellent, and we were all very impressed.'[8] Impressed enough to get the young man an office and funding to have a go at building M-Net.

But there was plenty of pitching left to do. The minister in charge of broadcasting, for one, needed to be convinced. 'When he sat in my office and I hammered him with questions, he had a reply to every one,' Pik Botha, minister of foreign affairs as well as broadcasting, told an interviewer years later.[9]

Vosloo had, of course, tested the waters, but Bekker did the rest to charm the cabinet veteran, who commended the young man for doing his background work very thoroughly. 'I have not come across a person in my life who was so determined, so intensely focused on a project as Koos Bekker was on this one. He would allow nothing to distract him. Come hell or high water, he wanted it and he got it,' recalled Botha.[10]

As noted previously, Botha suggested that Bekker and Vosloo should pull in more press groups to form a consortium, which they duly did. Together they then vied with the other contenders for the broadcasting licence. This included a presentation to the committee responsible for making a recommendation to government.

Hotel and casino boss Sol Kerzner and tech tycoon Bill Venter were the favourites, Arrie de Beer, a member of the committee, recalled years later. 'Then one day Koos Bekker walks in and puts in a performance!'[11] It made all the difference.

At that time there was a lot of uncertainty about whether the press groups could run a company supposedly focused on entertainment. News was their business, and news was the one thing they would not be allowed to provide on the pay channel. That is why others on the committee initially had high hopes for Kerzner with his casinos and movie theatres.

'Sol Kerzner ooh'ed and aah'ed, but that man Koos Bekker covered every possible angle and more,' De Beer remembered.[12] M-Net landed the licence.

According to Vosloo, Bekker never took any chances. Whenever they had to make submissions to the government, he practised with his team to the nth degree.[13]

'He would coach his top managers rigorously and have them do simulation exercises. He would then present the package to me as chair or to the relevant board committees. Once all the hitches had been pointed out and the finishing touches put to the strategy, Koos would go off into the lion's den,' writes Vosloo.[14]

Even when the business was up and running, Bekker kept pushing for more concessions to take the battle to the state broadcaster. 'We're continually imploring and lobbying government to relax our licence terms so that we can compete on a fairer basis with the SABC,' he told the *Financial Mail* in 1986.[15]

Remember how M-Net got the concession to run a free-to-air slot until it had signed up its break-even number of subscribers? That threshold was reached in 1988, but Open Time lasted until 2007. Bekker did a hell of a job keeping the authorities happy enough for long enough – not only when pitching to sitting governments, but also to those who may one day be in power.

Italy's Silvio Berlusconi might have started his career as a nightclub crooner, but by the late 1980s he had, according to Bekker, developed a knack for doing business, and was the first foreigner to whom Naspers exported technology.

Berlusconi had yet to run for public office. His controversial stints as prime minister still lay ahead, and he would refer to himself only much later as 'the Jesus Christ of politics'.[16] At the time Bekker pitched to him, the Italian was best known for his sprawling media empire, to which he was adding a pay-TV business called Telepiù.

'They met in the afternoon, and Koos worked through the night with a team in Milan and Johannesburg to deliver a proposal to Telepiù the next day,' recalls Cobus Stofberg.[17] Again, Bekker made the sale. Berlusconi bought the South African encryption technology.

This was only months before Italy hosted its second Soccer World Cup in 1990. It would be two decades before the tournament had its first final in Africa. And after losing the pitch for the 2006 final to Germany, South Africa simply could not miss out again.

Bidding for the biggest sporting event on the globe obviously has a long lead time. In 2004, South Africa was in the final throes of bidding for 2010.

But the final pitch ran into trouble when a film clip brought from home was first stitched into the presentation only hours before going live. An insider described the first showing of the film as 'an absolute shambles', the *Sunday Times* reported that weekend. Put more diplomatically, the video was deemed 'technically lacking, and needed to be altered'.[18]

So the Naspers boss, who was part of the bid committee, lent a hand. This time he had more than a pair of scissors – a whole media company was at his disposal.

'Such was the seriousness of the problem that SuperSport employees in Randburg were on stand-by to beam fresh images via satellite to the studio, with Naspers head Koos Bekker demanding that all company resources be on hand to work on the problem,' the *Sunday Times* reported.[19]

In this case the SABC had to work with its pay-TV rival to deliver the goods. And the presentation went well enough for the 2010 final to take place in a newly built stadium outside Johannesburg.

Back in the 1980s, the relationship with the state broadcaster had kicked off differently. Getting M-Net to break even so soon against an entrenched monopoly was one of Bekker's greatest feats. He and his team pitched the pay channel to households as an aggressive, challenger brand against the SABC, recalls then Y&R advertising executive Andrew Halley-Wright.

'So M-Net would be a full colour experience, not grey. It would be individualistic, not mass market; eventful, not every day; entrepreneurial, not bureaucratic – a brand, not a commodity; and not just any brand, but a challenger brand,' he adds.[20]

Many of M-Net's long-time staff believed the company had a deeper mission than merely attracting subscribers. Founded when a country, at war with itself, was not sure it could be a nation, the corporate culture stood out like a healthy thumb.

Remember the flat structure, the unassigned parking, the informal dress code and the first-name policy? It set the tone for what a business should look like in the new South Africa, says Vosloo. 'Bekker set the pace of how the public company in the new, coming South Africa would have to look. No discrimination whatsoever.'[21]

These days, this sounds like a low bar. But this was the 1980s, in a system slowly shedding its most draconian measures. The 'Rainbow Nation' was a long way off. 'So, in that sense, M-Net is the great pioneer that led us into the new South Africa,' Vosloo adds.[22]

The fledgling business did not have the legacy issues of, say, mining or banking or state-owned enterprises. It was a blank – and not *blanke* (white) – canvas. With M-Net one of the few success stories of the late 1980s, its impact as a new business was probably larger than would otherwise have been the case. The company was, after all, in show business – it showed what a business could look like.

Pitching is about landing a deal or making a business a success. But Bekker took it further, and positioned his ventures to last. This means he had to play a clever political game not only in the 1980s, when Naspers was close to government, but also in the years to follow. 'Why does a typical cell phone company succeed? It's because they've got the bloody licence. How do you get the licence? Politics,' he said in 2012.[23]

Bekker sees the media as the interface where politics and economics and regulation and technology meet. And bad politics is not good for business.

From his earliest days as CEO, he approached the history of Nasionale Pers – and particularly its historical association with the NP – in a way that can be best described as a Covid-19 strategy: it had to be masked and sanitised.

In 1998, when the company was rebranding itself for a different role in the new South Africa, Bekker wanted to give the company an entirely new name – probably, according to Vosloo, because he was sensitive about or even ashamed of its Afrikaner-nationalist past. But the board did not agree. A compromise was reached to 'rename' the company Naspers. It had in any case been listed under that shortened title since 1994, and it was already widely in use.

In 2000, after three years at the helm, Bekker noticed that *Die Burger* was commemorating its eighty-fifth anniversary with an exhibition of front pages from the past in the foyer of the Naspers Centre in Cape Town.

'It included several exultant newspaper posters that celebrated National Party election victories. Bekker immediately instructed the exhibition to be removed,' writes Vosloo.

This was as CEO. Years later, he would scupper a project of Vosloo's soon after taking over as chair.

'The most vehement disagreement in my relationship with Koos was about the publication of an official history of Naspers in celebration of the company's centenary in 2015,' Vosloo recounts.

By the time Bekker became chair, the book was far advanced, and Vosloo was acting as a sounding board for the author as he had more than four decades of personal, journalistic and management experience at the company.

The board had approved Vosloo's recommendation that Professor Lizette Rabe, head of the journalism department at Stellenbosch University, be commissioned to write the book. Under contract with Naspers, she had worked on the manuscript for four years when Bekker returned from his second sabbatical.

The book was to be published in Afrikaans and English. But Bekker summarily told Vosloo there would be no book at all.

Why would the new chair pull the plug on such an endeavour? Probably because he knew only too well that media companies are not just businesses with a commercial motive – they also play social roles, and usually have deeper cultural and even political missions. In the case of Naspers, this had been to further the cause of the Afrikaans language and the group who identified themselves as Afrikaners. *Die Burger* had been the official mouthpiece of the Kaaplandse Nasionale Party (the National Party in the old Cape Province, in line with the party's federal structure), and cabinet ministers had routinely served on its board. There was no denying the company's deep links to the government that had implemented apartheid.

A scroll through the 'history' section of the Naspers website gives some indication of Bekker's view of the company's past. First bullet: 'Naspers is founded in Stellenbosch, South Africa to produce a Dutch language newspaper'. Second bullet: 'Naspers adds book publishing to its operations and during the next 60 years grows into one of Africa's leading media groups'. Third bullet: 'M-Net founded, Naspers's first Pay TV business'. Then much more detail about recent transactions, conveniently skipping past the six decades in which Naspers helped the NP to nearly a dozen election victories.

No wonder Bekker refused to publish the company's official history. Business, after all, was more important.

'His reason was Naspers's thousands of black employees. If they were to read about the company's past, it would draw the attention of the ANC government to the company, which could be prejudicial to its regulated businesses, such as DStv and the digital expansions,' Vosloo explains.

Instead, what happened was an official apology for the role the company's publications had played during apartheid. Again, this was a clever piece of positioning. It was not Naspers that apologised, but its print subsidiary, Media24.

'We acknowledge complicity in a morally indefensible political regime and the hurtful way in which this played out in our newsrooms and boardrooms,' declared Media24 CEO Esmaré Weideman at a dinner celebrating the centenary of *Die Burger* and Naspers.[24] No book – just a sorry.

Vosloo believed Bekker's fears were exaggerated, and told him the company's history was public knowledge. 'So, too, was the reform we had brought about in the ranks of our own community from 1984 onwards.

This reform had culminated in the Afrikaans-speaking community's willing and hopeful integration into the new, democratic South Africa,' he writes.

The former chair even used his farewell speech to plead with Bekker to allow the book's publication. But by 2022 there was still no indication that it would ever see the light.

As mentioned in the previous chapter, Bekker reshaped Naspers into a useful tool to chase lucrative investments in media and later technology. Meanwhile, the original cultural mission of the company had conveniently been downgraded and delegated to smaller business units.

In some circles, Bekker is lauded for supporting Afrikaans. He gets much of the credit for the establishment of the channel kykNET, for example.

When the SABC became less enthusiastic about broadcasting content in his home language in the late 1990s, he instructed executives to explore the viability of hosting such a channel. 'He said, "see if you can make it work", but basically, "make it work,"' recalls Elize Malherbe, M-Net's director of special projects at the time.[25]

KykNET grew into one of the most successful platforms on DStv, branching out into ancillary channels and stimulating a host of local productions. It was, however, a viable enterprise in its own right as it had a well-defined market whose members were used to consuming video content in their home language. Two decades later, kykNET was hardly being carried by other parts of the business.

Commentators are less kind when it comes to Bekker's treatment of the print titles in the Naspers stable. By the 2020s, Media24 still published several magazines in Afrikaans, dozens of books a year, two dailies and a weekly. The original deal to have the profits from pay-TV support print, however, was not set in stone.

Over the years Naspers had transferred large amounts 'to extend the life of printed newspapers, even those that were already running at a loss as well as to move newspapers online', Bekker told *Fortunes* author Ebbe Dommisse.[26]

After 2019, MultiChoice was a separately listed entity, far removed from the surviving papers. Some believe that, whatever the corporate make-up of Naspers, print media is owed a historical debt for stumping up M-Net's start-up capital.

Ironically, *Volksblad* – the newspaper that Vosloo used to rattle PW Botha into accepting the concept of pay-TV – would survive deep into the 'new South Africa', only to disappear from news-stands in 2020 as Covid-19 took its toll on the economy.

Bekker was not about to swoop in and save a hundred-year-old title. Not as chair of the company that owned it. He is just not that emotional about it. A venture – whether a newspaper or a book about the history of the company – needed to make business sense, or at least sense for the business.

'It was never a personal issue for Koos, of that I am sure – merely an issue of viewpoint, policy and management,' concludes Vosloo.

Escaping a tarnished past, however, is no easy game. Decades after Naspers had officially severed its ties with the NP, the global news agency Reuters still described the company as 'an apartheid era newspaper publisher turned tech giant'.

Does Bekker's manoeuvring to obscure the less-than-glorious elements of the past mean he is always diplomatic? Certainly not.

For years, he criticised the tardy pace at which government was rolling out the infrastructure needed for higher internet speeds. He was also clearly no fan of South African competition authorities' approach to technology businesses.

'The competition people need to somehow lift themselves to a global level, otherwise they actually retard investment,' he told Naspers shareholders in 2019.[27] This was not long after a deal to acquire WeBuyCars was blocked by the authorities.

His approach has also guaranteed that he is hardly loved or even liked in the corridors of power. And boy, has he riled up some ANC cabinet members.

Former communications minister Yunus Carrim was not charmed by Bekker at all. When testifying at the Zondo Commission into state capture, he admitted to getting so angry during one of their discussions about digital encryption in 2013/4 that he had sworn at Bekker.[28]

In 2015, trade and industry minister Rob Davies opened fire after Bekker had complained in interviews that South Africa 'had no economic policy', that government departments weren't singing from 'the same hymn sheet' and that policy incoherence was hampering investment.

Davies took out a full-page advertisement in *Business Report* claiming that investment had only dropped marginally that year and that the trend over five years was 'unambiguously upwards'.

In the ad, the minister snarkily called Bekker a 'billionaire wine farmer'. That, the financial journalist Rob Rose wrote in a *Sunday Times* editorial, 'is sort of like referring to Warren Buffett as a wealthy bridge enthusiast from America's sleepy Midwest town of Omaha, who likes investing, reading newspapers and long walks around the Henry Doorly Zoo'.[29]

As zookeeper at Naspers, Bekker was willing to rattle a few political cages, but he was not keen to talk about apartheid, the elephant in the room.

Cowardice or foresight? Tough to tell. Considering his stance that white guilt for past transgressions should not attach to young South Africans, he may have been playing a long game. He may not necessarily have hoped that Naspers's past will disappear, perhaps more that it will fade into insignificance when South Africa and the world zooms in on the next big thing. In a time of rapidly evolving technology and new investment opportunities, he developed a strategy for finding that big thing. It involved spaghetti.

6.

IDENTIFY WALLS FOR SPAGHETTI

'The group internet approach is basically to throw spaghetti against the wall as fast as possible, and some pieces stick and some pieces fall off.'

– KOOS BEKKER, 2011[1]

'Our biggest success actually in China was that we failed so early and so spectacularly, and that caused a certain humility in us to change our policy.'

– KOOS BEKKER, 2016[2]

I N THE LATE 1970S, CHINA'S GOVERNMENT LED BY DENG XIAOPING, selected a settlement of some 300 000 people at the mouth of the Pearl River as one of four 'special economic zones' (SEZs). Shenzhen got the nod thanks to its proximity to Hong Kong, one of Asia's most important financial centres, which was still administered by Britain at that time.

Each of the other three SEZs was also only a short hop from more developed areas on China's border: Zhuhai was next to Macau, then governed by Portugal, and Shantou and Xiamen were on the doorstep of Taiwan. In Communist China, the four cities were havens where businesses could dip a toe in the waters of capitalism.

Today, Shenzhen has more high-rises than New York – a decent enough benchmark when assessing whether a city has arrived on the world stage.

The Seafront Towers are twin high-rises of thirty-nine and fifty storeys respectively. Linked by three sky bridges, these state-of-the-art buildings house Tencent's 12 000 employees. Inside you'll find all the amenities that can be expected from a tech giant – a basketball court, a swimming pool, a hall of billiard tables, and much more. And, of course, plenty of space and equipment on which to grind out the latest innovation.

When Hans Hawinkels first met Ma Huateng, the surroundings were less auspicious. The meeting took place in an office above a warehouse at the turn of the century.

Known as Pony Ma, because his name translates as 'horse', the Shenzhen local was running a popular instant messaging platform called QQ. Sporting nearly 20 million users, he needed help to take the business to the next level. Ma was part of a young team that had founded Tencent in 1998, but thus far it had only made losses.

As its logo, the company had two penguins. And the name was a combination of the Chinese characters 'teng' (腾), the last part of Ma's name, and 'xun' (讯), the second part of Runxun, a company he had worked for.[3] It could be anglicised nicely to Tencent. From Mandarin it translates as 'rise' or 'soar' and 'news', but more idiomatically it means 'galloping message'.[4]

One of Tencent's early backers had put a portfolio of fifty investments up for sale, and Hawinkels was in Shenzhen to look Ma's company over. He liked what he saw. Fortunately for Naspers, Ma and his team were unhappy with their current investors and wanted a stable strategic partner, Hawinkels recalled in 2021.[5] But why was this South African in China to start with?

Shortly after taking the reins at Naspers, Koos Bekker appointed Hawinkels as CEO of MIH Asia. His main task was to look for investment opportunities in the Far East. Bekker had identified China as a great wall (Great Wall, even) at which to throw spaghetti.

'The focus for the Hong Kong office was to look for opportunities both in Pay-TV and also for those in the rapidly developing internet sphere,' recalls Charles Searle, chief of Naspers's listed internet assets.[6]

But China was a risky play. By 2001, Naspers had already sunk $80 million (more than R500 million) into deals Hawinkels and his team had brought to the table. Compared to the billions Naspers would deploy in the 2010s and early 2020s, this sounds like peanuts. At the time, however, the Naspers market cap was languishing in the region of R4 billion, so having $80 million go to zero was a substantial hit. A Beijing-based internet service provider called Maibowang accounted for half of the losses, but the financial portal Eefoo and the sports portal Sports.cn also burnt cash.

'The executive management team (at MIH and Naspers) had reservations about investing in Tencent. Most of them were against putting more money into Chinese internet ventures,' Hawinkels recounted later.[7]

Naspers was about to report the first annual loss in its history, and here the company's man in the Far East wanted to pile more money into China. In the meantime, the dotcom crash was unfolding like a Greek tragedy. There was a sense of urgency, however, as other investors were also snooping around, remembers Searle.

'I was adamant that it was a good opportunity,' said Hawinkels. 'And Koos was able to convince the team that we should invest.' So, Naspers, through MIH, forked out R266 million (some $33 million) for 46,5 per cent of Tencent. As part of the agreement, the company also gave Tencent an R8 million cash injection.

'It was a credit to our board that they committed the last of the group's available cash resources on this high-risk investment,' says Searle, who has since also been a long-time Tencent board member.[8]

Naspers bought some shares from Ma and the other Tencent founders. The bulk of the stake, however, was acquired from two venture capital businesses: Millennium Vocal Group, a unit of Hong Kong-based telecoms company PCCW, and IDG Technology Venture Investments (now part of IDG Capital). Let's just call them PCCW and IDG.

Both were invested in Tencent for less than eighteen months. Each had paid $1,1 million for a 20 per cent stake. It was IDG that had put that portfolio of fifty investments up for sale. According to Hawinkels, it was happy to exit in 2001, but on condition that PCCW sell out too.

This proved to be a problem. For months, Hawinkels kept trying to get the telecoms provider to sell. PCCW had a new boss, the billionaire Richard Li, who according to Searle was not keen to exit. Li was actually interested in getting a larger stake in Tencent. Fortunately for Naspers, the dotcom crash put the squeeze on both IDG and PCCW, which moved Li to reconsider.[9]

Hawinkels, by his own admission, was persistent. Eventually, his counterpart at PCCW offered him the stake at a company valuation of $66 million – 'no due diligence, take it or leave it,' he recalls.[10] Naspers took it.

'We were very lucky,' the late Antonie Roux, then CEO of MIH's global internet business, remarked in 2006. 'Tencent was looking for a final round of funding. We had an opportunity to buy a stake in what was then a privately held company. We bought in when they were just starting to gain traction [with QQ].'[11]

The timing was incredible. MIH made the deal early in June 2001; by the end of that month Tencent was breaking even for the first time. Profits soon followed.

The sheer size of China's population, estimated at 1,27 billion when Naspers acquired its Tencent stake, and nearly 1,45 billion by 2022, piques the interest of many an investor. Bekker was attracted not only by the size of the market, but also by the potential of the nation itself.

'In terms of geography, Koos was keen on China, pointing out that in recorded history, China was more often the leading economy in the world than any western country, and predicting that the historical pattern would recur,' Searle remembers.[12]

In the two decades since 2001, China's economy has increased tenfold, and its gross domestic product (GDP) per capita is nine times higher. Bekker has also often praised the Chinese work ethic and the quality of its managers and engineers.

Ma and his co-founders exemplified this. At Tencent, they had different roles, and just looked like a really good team from the start, Hawinkels recalled in 2021.[13]

Interestingly, Tencent itself tosses more than the odd noodle in the direction of a room divider. And plenty of it has stuck. Two decades on, not much is left of the company's initial sources of revenue. Not only has it built the WeChat super app, but it has also sprawled into mobile gaming, financial services, social media, music streaming, and just about anything else that can be done profitably online.

The Tencent founders have all become billionaires several times over. And, as the title of this book suggests, Bekker too. Unfortunately for Hawinkels, it took a few years for Tencent – which to this day has a penguin as its logo – to prove itself as one of the tech world's greatest investments. And the losses in the rest of China hung around his neck like a whole other seabird.

His contract was not renewed after 2002 and he missed out on the long-term benefits. Hawinkels was a victim of 'Koos's guillotine', writes Vosloo rather frankly.[14]

Bekker's strategy since becoming Naspers CEO is often summarised as China and the internet. He actually had a more considered approach. Sure, he did not go much deeper into his old money spinner, believing that 'in pay TV the whole world was occupied', but the broadcasting businesses he had left were allowed to mature.[15]

Geographically, Bekker did not stick to China. More broadly, he latched onto the South African foreign policy *zeitgeist* of the early 2000s by taking a closer look at Brazil, Russia, India *and* China. If he was going to chuck spaghetti at a wall, it might as well be a BRIC wall.

Not only did these nations have large populations, growing middle classes and plenty of potential as consumer markets; due to differences in culture and language, they posed a major challenge to English-speaking investors.

'Where they feel uncomfortable is dealing with foreign languages and foreign cultures and cities that operate slightly differently from New York

City, so that's where we are at our best,' Bekker said to Moneyweb in 2009. 'So we'll go into Moscow long before they are there.'[16]

This was, of course, years before Russia's belligerent stance towards its neighbours became a problem for investors.

In 2006, Naspers paid $165 million for a 30 per cent stake in Mail.ru, Russia's most popular website, and an important portal for email and instant messaging. Soon after, Mail.ru expanded into social media and other consumer-facing internet services.

'What we like about Russia is the high growth rate of the economy and the excellent educational system. Russia has a pool of excellent engineers. They still lack certain infrastructure, but especially the cities are moving forward,' Bekker commented two months before putting ink on paper for the Mail investment.[17]

By the 2020s the company, which had renamed itself VK Group after its popular social networking site VKontakte, was still much stronger on its home turf than the global giant Facebook. Over the years, Naspers invested a further $500 million to retain its stake, but Russia's 2022 invasion of Ukraine had a devastating effect on Naspers's investment in the business (more in chapter 13).

In 2013, Naspers acquired a stake in Avito, Russia's largest classifieds platform. It later bought the entire business. Analysts often point to Avito as one of the best assets in the sprawling Naspers and Prosus portfolio of classifieds businesses. Early in 2012, Naspers CFO Basil Sgourdos valued it at $6 billion. In this investment too the war between Russia and Ukraine has complicated matters for Naspers (more in chapter 13).

In India, Bekker and his team window-shopped for years, but initially found the prices too high to acquire any company. In 2008, Naspers took the plunge and started an internet business called Ibibo from scratch. Bekker and his team formed a joint venture with Tencent to build the social network platform in such a way that it incorporates products such as instant messaging services, e-mail and online games into the Ibibo products. The company later pivoted to online travel, with its sites taking bookings for trips by air or bus and hotel stays in a nation of more than 1,2 billion people.

India was similar to South Africa, and Bekker liked it. 'You have pockets like Sandton in Bangalore ... and then you've got rural territories that are undeveloped, with no credit cards or literacy. We understand how to operate in those markets – in contrast to the Americans, who are scared to death of that,' he commented a few years prior to investing.[18]

In 2012, Naspers moved deeper into India, acquiring a 10 per cent stake in the e-commerce platform Flipkart for R858 million. The next year, the group pushed another R1,9 billion into the business, and invested a further R3,2 billion in a funding round the year thereafter. The backing helped Flipkart grow into India's largest online retailer. In 2017, Naspers invested another R1 billion. But when the world's largest retailer, Walmart, came knocking in 2018, Naspers sold its 12 per cent stake for a cool $2,2 billion (more than R30 billion).

'It's mainly also (about) choosing your competition. If we face up to Silicon Valley, there are companies there like Google, eBay and Yahoo! that are many times our size, and then frankly they just clobber us over the head and demolish us. They are probably better managed and better financed. So we try to fight in a field where we have a better chance of success,' Bekker said in 2009.[19]

In lusophone Brazil, Naspers paid $422 million for 30 per cent of a media company in 2006. Abril, a family-owned business, ran a portfolio of assets that looked very similar to the one Bekker had inherited at Naspers: print media, book publishing and pay-TV. Ever heard of Abril? Probably not, because it was the sort of bet management would prefer to forget. Abril could not be turned into a Naspers, not even by Naspers.

But the foray into Brazil brought Movile to Bekker's attention. A mobile phone services business that went through several iterations before settling on the name Movile, it would be the company that put food delivery on the menu for Bekker. In 2008, Naspers acquired a majority stake in Movile.

In 2013, through Movile, Naspers backed Brazil's iFood with $2 million, the first of a host of investments in the emerging trend of ordering food online and tracking the progress on a smartphone. By 2022, Naspers and Prosus had invested more than $7 billion in food delivery. As mentioned earlier, besides iFood, the portfolio included sizeable stakes in businesses such as Delivery Hero in Europe and Swiggy in India.

In a strange move for a CEO who was repositioning his media company for a future in which print would play a smaller role, Bekker took a punt on a few Chinese rags. Newspapers such as *Beijing Youth Daily*, *Titan Weekly* and *Xin'an Evening News* are mentioned in annual reports for a few years, but then disappear.

In the meantime, Tencent kept growing in the background. When Naspers first invested, the company had 20 million users on its QQ platform, but it wasn't earning a single cent. Soon the team clinched a revenue-sharing deal with China Mobile which would see Tencent rewarded for the traffic it generated via mobile users.

'[Y]ou know instant messaging (IM) was Tencent's origin – that was free PC to PC. So, when people went PC to mobile phone, they had to pay – some income started flowing in,' Bekker recalled in 2012.[20]

In Roux's opinion there was something fundamentally right about Tencent's business, and this had to do with IM. The long-lasting effects of the single-child policy the nation had introduced in the 1980s helped shape Chinese social media habits.

'IM, from early on, was seen as a social network. QQ originated out of the desire of the Chinese to communicate with one another,' he said in 2006.[21]

Over the years, Tencent has built a formidable social networking empire, adding a next generation of platforms with WeChat and Weixin to its QQ offering and constantly upgrading and improving on all three. By 2021, WeChat and Weixin together had nearly 1,23 billion monthly active users, and QQ almost 600 million.

As QQ grew from a few million to tens of millions and beyond, Tencent started doing good business out of providing its users with mobile games.

In other Asian markets, gamers played on consoles – think of Nintendo, Sony's PlayStation and later Microsoft's Xbox – which often meant buying a cartridge or a compact disc and inserting it into a machine at home. China was different from Japan and South Korea, and would develop its own consumer electronics habits.

'If you play console games, you don't meet other people,' said Roux.[22] Kids from small families craved social interaction, even if it was only on a screen, he reckoned. So the Chinese latched onto online games.

By the 2020s, investment analysts regarded Tencent as the global leader in online gaming, a reputation it has cemented with a number of blockbuster titles such as Honor of Kings, PlayerUnknown's Battlegrounds and Fortnite.

Big in games, yes, but Ma is hardly a one-trick pony. Over the past decade his company has diversified into a host of internet-based technology ventures, and by 2021 it was raking in more than a quarter of its revenue from fintech and business services, which covers anything from loan origination to cloud conferencing. Online advertising, for example, accounted for 17 per cent of revenue.

In effect, the company managed over two decades to build an entire habitat in which Chinese consumers live their social, professional and economic lives.

With Tencent chugging along nicely, Bekker's team could continue with his broad theme of investing in e-commerce in emerging markets. For the former M-Net boss, this had a familiar feel.

'E-commerce is a little bit like Pay-TV – it requires good systems, lots of people, heavy interaction with the public, and computer-assisted activities,' he said in 2012.[23]

But Bekker was willing to deviate from his theme if the asset seemed attractive enough. Sometimes it wasn't e-commerce *in* emerging markets, but e-commerce *or* emerging markets.

This helps to explain the acquisition of Abril in Brazil, and Bekker's foray into Chinese print media. Though these were not on the cutting edge of e-commerce, at least they were located in the right markets. And, as in the case of Brazil, these sorts of ventures could serve as introductions to the market and other lucrative businesses for Naspers to invest in.

'The cost of throwing spaghetti is very low,' he told Anton Harber. 'Then, if you see you get traction on something, you add five engineers, and then, if it works better, you add 30 engineers; you resource success and kill failure.'[24]

Similarly, there was no hard and fast rule against investing in more developed markets. In 1998, Naspers ventured into the United States by letting MIH take a stake in the software business OpenTV. Both Bekker and MIH CEO Cobus Stofberg waxed lyrical about the potential of the company and the new phenomenon of interactive television.

OpenTV's business was to supply the operating system that allowed viewers to download broadcasts, such as the electronic programme guide used by DStv, onto decoders. As a result, it entered into partnerships with broadcasters, of which DStv was one, and had licensing agreements with a number of digital receiver manufacturers around the world.

The future, according to Stofberg, lay in accessing services such as banking, the internet, home shopping, interactive games and more with a decoder from the comfort of your living room.[25] Looking back from the 2020s, it sounds like he was describing a smartphone.

In 1999, MIH invested more in OpenTV to bring its stake to 80 per cent (more about this in the next chapter).

The American endeavour was big, but even bigger was the R15,3 billion Naspers forked out for a Polish e-commerce business in 2008. Though based in Poznan, Tradus actually operated online auction and fixed-price sales sites in twelve European countries.

'When you are negotiating, people put on their most positive side, so you are never sure what you have bought. But now we have walked in the door as the new owners, we like what we see,' Bekker said in 2008.[26]

Naspers soon reorganised the business into two segments, focusing the Allegro platform on Eastern Europe and the Ricardo platform on the more developed markets of Western Europe. 'Tradus is like eBay – in other words, it connects two consumers to each other, the one buying a 3-Series

BMW and the other selling it, and it provides all the services you need to make the sale,' Bekker explained in 2008.[27]

When it comes to online classified businesses, it's often a winner-takes-all scenario. Each market tends to prefer a single dominant platform. 'You don't want to sell your car on the second platform but on the biggest one,' Bekker added.[28]

Though eBay soon came snooping around those markets, Ricardo retained its top spot in Switzerland until Naspers sold the business for $248 million in 2015. Allegro was still number one in Poland when it was disposed of for $3,2 billion in 2017.

In 2010, the year soccer legend Diego Maradona so memorably paced the sidelines as Argentina's manager during the FIFA World Cup held in South Africa, Bekker backed another Argentinian manager. Naspers invested R1 billion in OLX, the online classifieds business (mentioned in chapter 4) started by Alec Oxenford.

Though his first market was India, Oxenford ran the business from his hometown of Buenos Aires. From its founding in 2006 until Naspers invested, OLX (short for OnLine eXchange) had also established a strong foothold in Latin America and Portugal. Naspers would use OLX as its go-to brand for customer-to-customer trade, and expand its reach to 41 markets.

'Gradually we realised that our ability is in e-commerce, and we are focusing more and more on that,' said Bekker in 2012.[29]

Clearly, Bekker and Naspers threw plenty of spaghetti. But what stuck in the end? In India, Flipkart was an excellent investment, and sold at a substantial profit. Before 2022, the investments in Russia were seen as good bets. The arrival of Facebook Marketplace hardly had an impact on Avito – in sharp contrast with many classifieds businesses in less Russian parts of the world. But economic sanctions will at best complicate the stakes in Avito and VK Group, at worst make them worthless.

It will probably only become clear later in this decade whether the large business segments established in food delivery, classifieds, online payments and edtech will deliver satisfactory profits.

Bekker often receives the credit for zooming in on China. Strangely, though, during his tenure Naspers only made a single successful investment in the world's most populous nation. And its success probably means that Naspers or Prosus will avoid investing there again in the foreseeable future. 'We are not going to go into China, to be clear. We can't allocate capital in China better than Tencent can,' Sgourdos said in 2021.

'Tencent is our China play,' he said, adding that this was not due to an agreement, but 'just a choice that we made'.[30]

Tencent, nevertheless, is the best example of Bekker choosing a theme, picking a market, finding a company and investing. By 2021, the income Prosus received in Tencent dividends alone was more than ten times as much as Naspers's original investment.

But even when a business sticks, it is often the investor that does not stick it out long enough.

7.

HOLD ON WHEN YOU HAVE SOMETHING GREAT

'We invested in Tencent when it was a 30-person company. It now employs 11 000 people. We frankly don't want to cash in.'   – KOOS BEKKER, 2009[1]

'In some parts of the internet, let's say e-commerce, it's quite clear. You take a long time to build a business and then it is a viable, stable thing.'

      – KOOS BEKKER, 2010[2]

F OR VENTURE CAPITALISTS, A TYPICAL INVESTMENT HORIZON IS five to seven years. The idea is to find an exciting start-up, see it achieve scale, and sell, pocketing the profit.

During Bekker's time as Naspers CEO, the company did not sell a single share in its most lucrative investment: the Chinese tech champion Tencent. Holding on for that long is unusual.

'We [Naspers] were advised to sell our stake in 2004, when shares in Tencent were worth one Hong Kong dollar,' Bekker stated at the Naspers annual shareholders' meeting in 2017. 'Five years ago, there was agitation to sell at HKD 45, and again today at HKD 325, people want us to sell. We think the price is going up, and that this is the best opportunity for our cash at the moment.'[3]

By then, he was chair of the Naspers board, and no longer ran the company on a day-to-day basis. True to form, Tencent's share price more than doubled in the four years that followed. (It has since given up some of those gains.)

Naspers shareholders were nervous for a reason. Some of them had watched previously as Bekker and his team latched onto a promising tech investment, only to hold on for too long.

OpenTV was the prime example. Naspers, through MIH, backed the American technology company with hundreds of millions of rands. In the late 1990s it looked like a clever piece of vertical integration – after all, DStv was one of OpenTV's clients.

This start-up was seen as a global leader in interactive TV. It built the software for digital set-top boxes, and developed applications for use by pay-TV broadcasters. The e-commerce platform OpenTV had set up for British Sky Broadcasting (BSkyB) was an early example. By the turn of the century it had also signed up other pay-TV businesses such as TPS in France, Via Digital in Spain, Senda in Sweden, Stream in Italy and EchoStar's DISH Network in the United States.

Financial journalists speculated that television could replace the personal computer as the main access point for the internet, and this helped fuel the market's optimism when the company listed on the Nasdaq in November 1999.

OpenTV shares were offered at $20, raising $150 million from investors and valuing the company at more than $600 million. This was at the height of the dotcom craze, so OpenTV shares rallied more than 200 per cent on the first day. MIH and Naspers had listed their first tech unicorn: a company valued at more than $1 billion.[4]

Its share price rocketed in the months that followed, peaking at $245. In March 2000, with a market cap of more than $5 billion, it acquired software maker Spyglass for $2,5 billion (in an all-stock deal).[5]

Naspers and MIH controlled this unicorn and owned more than 37 per cent, of its economic value. But OpenTV was not profitable. It was bleeding cash on development costs and was vulnerable to competitors with deep pockets, such as Microsoft. Interactive TV's future was also far from certain, and depended on widespread adoption.

Then, of course, the dotcom bubble burst. 'We are concentrating on operating and building the business. The dotcom fall-out needn't worry us. It may be an opportunity to buy cheap properties,' MIH CEO Cobus Stofberg told the *Financial Mail* in 2001.[6]

Or to sell your own asset cheaply. The next year, Bekker and Stofberg offloaded the stake in OpenTV for $185 million (then R1.9 billion). This left investors smarting at the thought that had they sold earlier, billions more could have been pocketed.

Calling the peak is a guessing game, and Naspers under Bekker positioned itself as a long-term partner rather than a speculator that would flip an asset for a quick profit. But it still hurt.

The buyer was Liberty Media Corp., a business controlled by John 'Cable Cowboy' Malone. In the first year, Liberty Media wrote down nearly half of OpenTV, citing slower than expected growth in the interactive television industry and cutbacks by broadband service providers.[7]

Bekker and Naspers might not have sold OpenTV for the maximum, but they did realise a profit. And the less optimistic future of interactive TV was the next owner's problem. Still, Naspers shareholders saw billions being left on the table.

Then, in the rubble of the dotcom crash, it became clear that Naspers had found a star performer in China. Not only was Tencent growing users of its QQ chatting platform by the tens of millions, it had also found a way to earn revenue through a deal with mobile phone operators.

Naspers invested in June 2001. By the end of that year, Tencent was already reporting a modest profit of $1,2 million. The next year it paid its first dividend, and it has rewarded shareholders with distributions ever since. By contrast, Meta Platforms, which owns Facebook, WhatsApp and Instagram, has never paid a dividend.

On 16 June 2004, Tencent listed on the Hong Kong stock exchange at HKD 3,70 a share. This valued the company at HKD 6,2 billion (nearly $800 million or R5 billion) The stakes of both Naspers and the Chinese tech start-up's founders were diluted as they offered shares to the public. After listing, Naspers retained a holding of 37,5 per cent.

Before long, Tencent was worth more than $1 billion. Again, Bekker and his team had lassoed a unicorn.

'We invested about $30 million four years ago, and it's now worth about 20 times that amount. They employ about 2 000 people, and they're virtually all young. I think the oldest person is about 33, and they're developing some exciting products,' Bekker said in 2005.[8]

The listing in Hong Kong created a problem, however. As the share price was (and remains) readily known, it allowed investors to instantly place a value on Naspers's stake in Tencent. As the tech company's share price advanced on the Hang Seng Index, all sorts started watching, commenting and agitating, be they long-term backers, short sellers, financial journalists or even politicians.

Tencent was laying golden eggs, and just about everyone seemed to have a recipe for an omelette – or even a cooked goose.

Still, Bekker held on. Nearly a decade in, he believed Tencent had some way to go, as the company was profitable and at margins that were holding up well. '[In China] there's a huge audience, and if you simply collect a small amount from them efficiently with a low level of friction, then the figures pack up,' he commented in 2009.[9]

As a result of the one-child policy, the nation's birth rate had slowed, but that didn't mean the Chinese internet population would stagnate. He expected it to keep growing from about a quarter of the population to the Japanese and Korean levels of 80 per cent.

'So we think there's growth in the number of warm bodies on the internet ... But the RPU – the average revenue per subscriber – is also going up because people use more services and they're more prepared to pay for it,' Bekker added.[10]

He believed in China's potential, but also wanted to get a foothold in other places. So the full Tencent dividend was not passed through to Naspers shareholders. Instead, it was deployed to fund a host of e-commerce investments.

But Bekker overestimated the performance of the rest of the portfolio he was building. '[I]f you look at the long-term future, ten years from now, I think e-commerce will be by far our biggest unit,' he said in 2012. With five years of good growth, he believed the likes of OLX, Ibibo and Allegro could '(take) over from pay-TV and maybe even from the listed investments'.[11]

The listed investments were, of course, the mountain of value represented by Tencent and, at that stage, the molehill of Russia's Mail.

Though Bekker was bullish on Tencent, he nevertheless severely underestimated its growth. By early 2022, Tencent was ten times larger than a decade earlier, and still worth at least five times more than all the other Naspers (and by then Prosus) assets combined. This hardly sounds balanced.

In fact, Tencent did so well that it not only made Naspers lopsided, but it also created challenges on South Africa's stock market.

While Naspers's growth was certainly impressive in the years that immediately followed Tencent's listing in Hong Kong, it was not the only gig in town. The South African economy was still chugging along nicely, growing at more than 4 per cent a year. The mining companies listed on the JSE were benefiting from a global commodities boom, fuelled in large part by the rapid economic growth of China.

But in 2008, South Africa's fortunes changed. Electricity supply constraints became evident, and growth slowed suddenly as soon as 'load shedding' became part of the vocabulary. Business confidence suffered as rolling power cuts made it tougher for mining firms to supply platinum, iron ore, coal and gold to hungry markets in the rest of world. The global financial crisis later that year ruined the appetite for commodities almost completely, pummelling the rand against major currencies. The recession that followed ended a near decade-long consumer-spending bonanza.

The next decade would be one of stagnation under president Jacob Zuma. Policy uncertainty, indications of corruption on a grand scale, and weaker economic growth at home convinced many of South Africa's largest companies to look for acquisitions abroad. But the successes were few and far between.

Many businesses destroyed value by betting on developed markets, with the R21 billion Woolworths acquisition of Australia's Dow Jones a prime example.[12] Others overpaid for ventures in lucrative but volatile markets, such as Nigeria, where Tiger Brands forked out R1,5 billion for a majority stake in Dangote Flour Mills, only to sell it for $1 three years later – and no, $1 is not a typo.[13]

The JSE's two stand-out successes after the global financial crisis were the no-frills bank Capitec and, of course, Naspers.

Between 2008 and 2018, Capitec's market cap grew from about R3 billion to more than R100 billion. Naspers ballooned from R60 billion to more than R1 200 billion in the same period. Capitec's success was a local story as it gained millions of clients from more established financial institutions with its thrifty business model. By contrast, Naspers was all China.

During the Zuma years, South Africa in many respects turned into an economic basket case, with most of its fundamentals – infrastructure, human capital and competitiveness – going in the wrong direction. Yet the country's net international investment position (NIIP) somehow improved.

This was as a result of 'valuation changes', according to a 2018 research note by Reserve Bank economists Bojosi Morule and Daan Steenkamp.[14] Though they did not spell this out, Naspers's rally on the back of Tencent represented the only shift large enough to account for the improvement.

By 2018, South Africa actually compared favourably to other emerging markets despite a large deficit on its current account, the economists wrote. So one success managed to compensate for an entire economy's woes.

In fact, Naspers did so well following the global financial crisis that the company effectively outgrew the JSE. When Bekker took the reins in 1997, Naspers represented less than 1 per cent of the stock exchange's total value. When he stepped down as CEO in 2014, the company accounted for slightly more than 5 per cent of the JSE's value, largely thanks to Tencent's growth. But by 2018 the Chinese company's continued run had propelled Naspers to a market cap of more than R1 trillion, representing a whopping 25 per cent of the JSE's shareholder weighted index.

The largest players on most stock exchanges are institutional investors such as pension funds and other asset managers. As they deal with retirement savings, they are not inclined to bet the farm on a single investment. They build diversified portfolios and are usually bound either by statutory regulations or self-imposed rules to not hold more than, say, 10 per cent of their funds in one stock.

Naspers has been a blessing and a curse for South Africa's asset managers. In sharp contrast with much of the rest of the bourse, it has delivered remarkable returns over nearly two decades. Unfortunately, this means it has also consistently become too large a part of many institutional investors' portfolios. So these asset managers have constantly been forced to sell Naspers stock as soon as it represents more than a certain threshold of their holdings.

Imagine the frustration for a long-term investor of having to let go of your best performer, only to see it do even better the next year and the year after next.

Shorter-term investors also have gripes. From 2015 onwards, Naspers started trading at an ever-larger discount to the value of its stake in Tencent. Simply put: in 2017, when Naspers was worth $85 billion, its stake in Tencent was worth more than $110 billion. This means in effect that the market ascribed a negative value to the rest of Naspers's assets!

Many analysts, and CEO Bob van Dijk too, believed Naspers and Prosus traded at a large discount due to this phenomenon of 'forced selling' by asset managers.

Other commentators are less kind, saying that the company has been destroying value for nearly a decade by allocating capital badly and incentivising management the wrong way.

Many have argued that Naspers, and now Prosus, should unbundle the Tencent stake to unlock value for shareholders.

In June 2011, Bekker told Moneyweb's Alec Hogg: 'I think having worked with investors over the years, at least, investors in us, what they do is the following: They say, okay, you've got a stake in Tencent, it should be worth, let's say R100 a share, if I'm so keen on Tencent I'll go and buy Tencent shares, I get them as a parcel, in your case. So, I won't give R100 for them, I'll give you R80 for them. In other words, I'll discount it by 20 percent, and then your Mail stake, I'll discount that by 30 percent. So, when they make up the package, they actually put in Tencent at a discount, Mail at a discount, everything at a discount, and that's how they come to the present value.'[15]

Back then he was almost philosophical about it, adding that his team did not get very excited about ups or downs in the short term. Over longer periods it depended more on the quality of earnings that could be delivered. 'If you deliver, you should get value; if you don't deliver, you'll get fired,' he said.

But that was before the deluge of criticism in the years that followed. As Tencent kept running, with Naspers tagging along, the difference between the Chinese superstar and the rest of Bekker's asset pool became all too clear. Naspers's share price was climbing, but Tencent's was climbing faster. So the discount widened. Investors started pushing the Naspers management and board to take steps to narrow this discrepancy.

Some things could not be helped. Naspers was founded in South Africa, headquartered in Cape Town and listed on the JSE. Therefore, as part of the investment case in the company, the country's political risk played a role. Those were the Zuma years. Banks were bullied for following the rule book in closing the accounts of politically connected individuals and businesses. Finance ministers were not secure in their jobs. It all weighed on the Naspers share price in some form.

Also, despite the best efforts by management to package the company as having a consistent strategy, many investors saw Naspers as a stitch-job of disparate assets in very different parts of the world.

'Some people are obsessed with the idea that the share trades at a discount to the parts. Most composite companies run at a discount.

In the last five years the big four (Facebook, Amazon, Netflix and Google), which are all composites, have outperformed the market by 120 percent,' said Bekker, then board chair, in 2017.[16]

His tone had changed. By then, his successor's generous remuneration package was also in many investors' crosshairs. More than a few resented the idea that such a large part of Van Dijk's compensation should be linked to the Naspers share price, which was largely driven by Tencent's performance. No one wanted to see a new chief executive getting a free ride.

Clearly, Bekker was exasperated by the criticism and the nagging calls to unlock value. 'The argument for breaking up Naspers is completely illiterate,' he declared at that year's annual general meeting.[17]

In the half-decade that followed, however, the company took several steps to try to reduce the discount, and rejigged the pay packages of top executives in an attempt to appease shareholders.

Having not let go of a single Tencent share since investing, Naspers sold 2 per cent in 2018. The move raised $10 billion that was mostly ploughed into its e-commerce segments in online classifieds, food delivery, payments and edtech. The company also disposed of its stake in the Indian company Flipkart and used the proceeds for the same purpose: to beef up the e-commerce portfolio, and reduce debt in those businesses to more manageable levels. Naspers then bundled the e-commerce investments together along with the remaining stake it held in Tencent – around 31 per cent – for a listing on the Euronext exchange in the Netherlands.

The name Prosus was chosen for the new company, in which Naspers retained a stake of nearly 73 per cent. Prosus means 'forwards' in Latin, and the P-word was tested in 104 languages to ensure it did not connote anything inappropriate.

Naspers retained its primary listing on the JSE and remained headquartered in Cape Town, but Prosus only had a secondary listing in Johannesburg and was based in Amsterdam. The boards and top management teams of Naspers and Prosus were close to identical.

The listing in September 2019 attracted plenty of interest. European investors were starving for tech stocks and, so the reasoning went, exposing them to such a mix of e-commerce assets would stimulate constant buying of Prosus stock and close the discount.

The move was not a silver bullet, though. Tencent's share price advanced further, and one discount turned into two – Naspers traded at a discount to its stake in Prosus, and Prosus was worth less than its own Tencent shares.

And so, in 2021, Prosus disposed of another 2 per cent of Tencent, netting a further $15 billion. This was only weeks after a lock-up period barring the company from selling Tencent stock had expired. Most of this second tranche of cash was spent on further acquisitions in online payments and edtech, as well as a sizeable share buy-back scheme.

Starting in 2021, Prosus undertook not to let go of Tencent stock for three years. But this created the expectation that it would sell more Tencent shares as soon as it could, analysts said.

It would do so even sooner than that. In June 2022, with the discount gaping at between 50 and 60 per cent, Naspers and Prosus announced an 'open-ended' share repurchase programme. Prosus started selling Tencent stock in small batches, using the proceeds to buy back Naspers and Prosus shares. This happened after consultations with the Chinese company's management. Though Van Dijk kept mum on how long his team would employ the strategy, it could sell down as much as 2 per cent of Tencent per year, raising $10 billion in the process. Early indications were that the plan was indeed narrowing the discount.

This move seemed at odds with Bekker's earlier thinking. 'We want to be a stable partner. We won't dip out simply because we think we could buy the shares next month at a cheaper price,' Bekker said in 2009. 'Plus, Tencent also teaches us quite a lot.'[18]

By holding on to Tencent, Naspers gained more than just the investment returns in the form of capital appreciation and dividends. It formed a relationship with the Chinese company and its management team, a group at the cutting edge of technological development.

Naspers injected $1 million in cash into Tencent in 2001. It was part of the deal when acquiring shares in the company. The investor also received two seats on the board. Since Tencent's listing, these were filled by Charles Searle and Antonie Roux. When Roux passed away in 2012, Bekker took his place.

'We have assisted them with top-level stuff, but can't take credit for what they have achieved. We can't even speak the language,' Roux told the *Financial Mail* in 2006.[19] The 'top-level stuff', of course, is very important if a company wants to transition from the early stages of development to a listed entity.

'[T]hey picked us because they needed us to help them with certain things: to get to scale, to become a public company, to put in the right governance frameworks, all those type of things. To help them think a bit about the future,' said Naspers and Prosus CFO Basil Sgourdos.[20]

As Tencent grew, not only in size but also in confidence, it gave Naspers plenty to think about in turn. As early as 2002, the South African investor started licensing some of Tencent's technologies for use in other markets such as Thailand, Indonesia and sub-Saharan Africa.

'[I]n the development of the technology and the use of the technology outside of China, we increasingly work together with Tencent in doing that,' Stofberg said in 2007.[21]

One example is Ibibo, Naspers's first venture in India. Three years in, Bekker noted that the company had taken some pain, and learnt some lessons. 'Tencent is bringing their engineering power, and we have a 50/50 venture, and if it works out I think we'll be able to play a major role in the internet there.'[22] It sounds a bit like Tencent to the rescue ...

Years later, there is still some cross-pollination. Though there was a friendly relationship at the highest level – among others via those two board seats – there was also cooperation lower down, said Sgourdos.

'Think about it – ten years ago, Tencent was just a gaming and social networking company. They had no e-commerce, they had no payments.' Naspers started investing in those areas ahead of the Chinese giant.

'We saw some things, we learned some things and we liked them. Obviously we don't tell Tencent what to do – they are a very capable and competent management team, and they stand on their own two feet,' Sgourdos said.

E-commerce and fintech now represent a substantial part of Tencent's earnings. But Naspers and Prosus are probably the ones learning more these days.

'We did not see food delivery for the first time in some country where we landed up and ordered food. We adopted it from China. From Tencent. From their investment in Meituan. They opened our eyes up to it,' Sgourdos added.

Analysts regard China's Meituan as a world leader in the field. Naspers and Prosus has since piled more than $7 billion into food delivery platforms.

And there are examples, such as Flipkart, where Naspers and Tencent have co-invested. So, holding on to the greatest tech investment of the century so far also had the benefit of helping Naspers find options for diversification beyond Tencent.

Still, in early 2022, Naspers, through Prosus, was still the largest shareholder in Tencent. And its stake, even if somewhat diminished due to China's toughening stance on big tech (more in chapter 13), was worth a whopping R3 trillion. Though its value is a moving target, Bekker's comment from a decade earlier still seemed appropriate: 'We are not married to the share, but at this point in time it's paying shareholders.'

The executive team had the ability to understand the investment's potential and managed the relationship with Tencent extremely well over the years, says veteran analyst and investor Kevin Mattison. 'Naspers, until recently, has kept a firm grip on that stake. They did extremely well not to sell, despite constant pressure from investors to unlock value.'[23]

To achieve this, Bekker as CEO needed to take charge and be in control.

8.

TAKE CHARGE

'do something you like
if it's an office job
remember who's the boss
and who's in charge
and that you're the latter'
FROM 'WALK FAST, WHISTLE' – TOAST COETZER
(THE BUCKFEVER UNDERGROUND)

'If the entrepreneur, let's say, is much older than the rest
or much richer than the rest or whatever, it tends to produce a type of a leader-follower structure, and it doesn't
work in media.'   – KOOS BEKKER, 2008[1]

T HE DREAM OF BEING YOUR OWN BOSS CONVINCES MANY
an entrepreneur to take the plunge. But going it alone often means
managing a host of complex relationships – with outside investors, risk-
conscious financial institutions and/or vicious competitors – that can
crush that feeling of freewheeling independence.

Bekker engineered a career that gave him many of the advantages of
being an entrepreneur without having to deal with some of the downsides.
This enabled him to take charge of his time, his work and the enterprises
he managed. He could concentrate his efforts on lucrative endeavours and

passion projects. As a result, he had more of a say in his own destiny than most of his contemporaries.

'My work is interesting ... we do business in 130 countries in the world, I fly to interesting places, I drink expensive wine, I talk to interesting politicians. It's a wonderful life,' he told an interviewer in 2014.[2]

That was, of course, after years at the helm. In a far earlier interview, he remarked that his job as managing director was 'not especially important ... All I do is to create an environment in which people can do their best and I then try to bind them together,' he said shortly after M-Net's first broadcast in 1986.[3]

And he used a clever strategy to achieve this. The new company had an informal dress code and a flat hierarchy. 'Your parking space ... was first come, first served,' recalls M-Net veteran Jock Anderson. 'The CEO didn't say, this is my spot.'[4]

Bekker positioned himself as a 'cool' boss, unaffected by power. Hierarchy was so 'last season'. In hiring staff for the pay-TV business, he was interested in the best guys in the industry, not in the best guys' bosses, he would say.[5]

But it was about more than the possible benefits of a relaxed atmosphere. This was long before insta-stories about cosy office environments or millennials blogging about the quality of the coffee at their place of work. So what was to be gained from positive PR? 'For us, informality actually had a business purpose,' he said later.[6]

One day, Richemont boss Johann Rupert called M-Net to 'speak to Mr Bekker'. Confusion ensued, as the switchboard operator did not know anyone who went by that name. Mr Bekker was only known as Koos.[7]

Bekker's business clearly stood out. 'People used to address their bosses by their surnames. The problem is when you have that sort of relationship, it's almost impossible to tell him that he's talking nonsense,' he says. Rupert later remarked that this was no way to run a company.[8]

But there was a deeper strategy at play in Bekker's renowned 'flat' management structure. It was not only about keeping bosses humble; he also reckoned that with people on a first-name basis, there was less of a barrier when managers needed to criticise the work of subordinates, a long-time colleague recalls.

In the short term, the benefits might be collegiality and good relations, but over decades there should be a compound effect. Spotting managers' mistakes early must surely be beneficial. And could constructive feedback from a senior, without fear of the *meneer* (sir), help accelerate development?

Bekker says he believes in picking good people, trusting them and delegating to them.[9] As managing director and CEO, he was decisive. He said either yes or no. In management meetings at M-Net, he would listen and wait until all the attendees had finished with their contributions. Then he'd say, '*manne* (chaps), let's do the following,' and list the action points on a whiteboard, says a former colleague.

This approach worked for him at M-Net, and he would also employ it at Naspers. 'Bekker does not suffer fools,' Media24 CEO Esmaré Weideman told Anton Harber in 2012. 'He is very soft-spoken, and does not raise his voice, but cuts through the crap very quickly. You can't bullshit him. If he expects you to deliver and you don't, you'll soon be out on your ear.'[10]

Soft-spoken, sure, but he did speak his mind. Shortly after Bekker took over as Naspers CEO, plans for a new building in Johannesburg to house the company's newspapers were presented to him, recalls former *Volksblad* editor Hennie van Deventer.[11]

'Without beating about the bush, he shot down the proposed design. It was a "horrible" building, according to him,' writes Van Deventer, who had scouted out the site as chief of the company's newspaper division at that time.

This was after months of input by Naspers directors and several compromises about the building's 'look and feel'. Bekker's response drove the architect to tears, and the design had to be changed drastically and at great cost. '*Ja-nee*, from the start the boss's word was law!' notes Van Deventer.[12]

He retired soon afterwards, and only saw 'Koos's building' (or Media Park as it was officially known) two decades later. In many ways it was an improvement on the original proposal, Van Deventer acknowledges.

As Naspers CEO, Bekker had specific ideas about how certain business units should run and which new projects they should try. Many initiatives that would otherwise not have been embarked upon went ahead because 'Koos sê so' (Koos says so). Colleagues later abbreviated this factor to 'KSS'.

These imperatives filtered down through the ranks. Sometimes, Bekker would even zoom in and take a personal interest. 'He was hands-on and had strong opinions,' wrote the late Matthew Buckland, who had interacted with Bekker from 2008 onwards while working at 24.com and News24, but later made a name as an entrepreneur.[13]

During this time, Bekker took News24 under his direct management for a while. It was early days for the consumption of news content on mobile devices and the CEO considered the site a major digital asset for Naspers, recalls Buckland.

Bekker then conducted an audit of the business by inviting staff members to his office one by one for a cup of tea. He was so unimpressed with the person responsible for News24's mobile site that he had him summarily dismissed.

'To give you an idea of how unusual this was, Koos was most likely about twenty positions above the mobile guy in the Naspers hierarchy – so senior, in fact, that most people in the mobile guy's position would have been unlikely ever to have met the CEO. His decision to fire the underling was about as hands-on as a CEO can get,' Buckland adds.

Despite his being at the helm of a multinational enterprise, Bekker immersed himself in the details of some very modest parts of the business.

He once asked Weideman if he could attend an editorial meeting at *Huisgenoot*. It is not the sort of table around which company strategy or even editorial policy is likely to be discussed, just the sad, sexy or smutty true-life dramas that fill the pages of the magazine each week.

Weideman obviously warned her troops to be at their best, as her boss's boss would be attending the meeting. 'We were nervous, but Koos sat there deathly quiet, taking notes as debates raged from this side to that. Eventually we forgot he was even there,' she recalls.[14]

Around 2006 Koos took an interest in the business pages of *Die Burger*. He wanted them to look more like the *Financial Times* or the *Wall Street Journal*, and a target of a predetermined number of broadsheet pages (eight, if the author's memory serves correctly) was set by the layers of managers between Bekker and the journalists on the ground. Unfortunately, the business section of a regional paper does not magically start producing volumes of stories to the standard of the *FT* or *WSJ*. Junior reporters stayed until late, translating reams of wire copy to fill those pages.

'Bekker is a slave driver in so far as he expects others to adhere to the same standards he sets himself. When there is work to be done, normal hours don't apply,' writes Ton Vosloo.

He recalls how, in the early 1990s, Dutch personnel complained bitterly that the boss was ruining their weekends. 'When we started with FilmNet in the Netherlands, our first international venture in 1991, Koos would often summon staff for a Saturday or Sunday conference.'[15]

Bekker scoffed at the idea of a shorter work week, limited to thirty-five hours by some European governments. And he balked at the notion of personnel being coddled by, for example, giving them the right not to have their email pile up while on leave.

Watch online speeches of the Naspers CEO, and later chair, and you might be surprised how often he chides the developed world for not having the same work ethic as China. The future for European children, he remarks, will likely be to flip hamburger patties in the Shanghai Hilton.

'If you ask me how many hours do I work [per week], I don't know, sixty, seventy, something. Do I resent it? Not at all, I love it,' Bekker said.[16]

Anton Harber recalls how he and a partner approached Bekker with an idea for a 'small but interesting' venture. 'He responded quickly, at some length, and invited us to fly down to Cape Town to discuss it. At that meeting, he was keen and committed, but had firm advice about how we should go about implementing our idea.'[17]

With hundreds of deals coming across his table every year, Bekker had to develop a method of filtering, of staying in charge of his time and effort.

'When we did not follow that advice to the letter, he stopped answering our emails. That was it. It was his way or nothing – and who is to argue when his way is so successful?' adds Harber.[18]

Most people don't argue. Or at least, they know when to dig in their heels and when to let it go. 'He appreciates people who stand up to him,' says Weideman. 'If you give good enough reasons, he will accept them.'[19]

But he does push his people hard, as long-time M-Net executive and more recent MultiChoice chair Nolo Letele can attest.

'[I]nvariably you were asked how long is this going to take to deliver, it might be a business plan or whatever and you say I'll have it within two weeks, three weeks and then he says fine, I want it on Monday ...' recalls Letele.[20]

Buckland had a similar experience when working for Bekker. In his case it was more of a pet project of the CEO than a big commercial venture. As a fan of literature and a keen writer of opinion pieces over the years, Bekker was behind the publishing of *Om te skryf,* an Afrikaans version of the industry classic *Writing Prose* by Thomas Kane and Leonard Peters. The book studies the writing styles of accomplished local and international authors and aims to teach the finer art of writing, specifically in Afrikaans.

Buckland, who says that Bekker's impatience was well known, led a team charged with designing a web app which would serve as the book's digital version.

'Midway through the project, Koos decided to bring the deadline forward by a week, which no client in my career had ever done before. But there was no use arguing. It was KSS, and this was Koos. We had no choice but to pull a rabbit out of a hat.'[21]

Sure, his image in the lower rungs of the business may have been that of the media mogul with unrealistic expectations. And 'KSS' was often seen less as a call to arms in newsrooms and more as a fad, to be followed in letter but not in spirit, in a declining industry. Reporters would comment cynically when taking delivery of the bags of mealies Bekker distributed from his farm every year as a gesture of goodwill. In later years these seasonal gifts would include punnets of plums from his Babylonstoren estate, which some journalists mocked as the fruits of their own labour.

But even those who might have been disaffected with him over the years will tell you that he was very much someone who took charge.

'If you head up a company, you can never give any of your subordinates that unconditional approval our mothers give us. You have to be able to fire anyone if that's what is needed to save the ship,' he himself says.[22]

Bekker was known to tell new appointees, especially in management, that they should not expect dinner party invitations from him. He wanted to keep them at a distance, in case he had to let that person go.

'My mistakes were mostly to be too late in responding to a crisis,' Bekker commented in 2014. 'An enterprise goes wrong, you try to fix it, you realise later you need to apply the chainsaw, but the leader tried hard and he's your friend. You give him another two months, but by then the floor is covered in blood and you need to let seventy people go, where earlier it would only have been thirty.'[23]

He nevertheless inspired intense loyalty from those who worked closely with him. Very few colleagues will say anything about him at all, let alone anything negative.

Bekker himself looks back fondly on some of the times he spent with the people he worked with. He says that friendships formed in a person's teens or twenties will eventually dissipate, but that bonds formed at the office are lasting and more meaningful.

Some of the most worthwhile moments of his career were spent drinking with colleagues in China or crying together over a deal that wasn't or to celebrate a success together, he says.

'To go drifting down the Bosphorus on a sailing boat, and drink white Sicilian wine ... It's one of the most unbelievable experiences I've had in my life, and it comes from colleagues.'[24]

And they still managed to get the job done.

M-Net co-founder and long-time Naspers director Cobus Stofberg praises Bekker for his work ethic, and says his old mate from university days would not hesitate to get his hands dirty.

This was true even if those hands, in later years, got dirty mostly on the screen of a smartphone. Buckland recalls how Bekker made specific and detailed suggestions about the *Om te skryf* web app's usability and functionality. 'This was a man in control of a trillion-rand empire, making user interface suggestions for one small app.'[25]

When it came to broader issues, Bekker also wanted to take charge. And he seemed committed to his method of bringing deadlines forward.

In 2006, Bekker received the Ernst & Young Entrepreneur of the Year Award and used the opportunity to have his say about black economic empowerment (BEE).

At that time, Naspers was cooking up BEE deals at its Media24 and MultiChoice subsidiaries. Conspicuously, the company was not concluding an empowerment deal at the group level as Naspers saw itself as a global operation with international investors. It saw BEE 'as a purely South African imperative', according to CFO Steve Pacak.[26]

This was the last years of Thabo Mbeki's presidency, and the economy was still chugging along nicely, growing at nearly 5 per cent a year. But as is often the case, the haves were benefiting more than the have-nots, and calls for stronger measures to enforce BEE – and make it more broad-based – grew louder. Bekker had a different idea.

'[D]rive it hard for a fixed period, say five years,' he suggested. He was one of a number of voices in the business community propagating a sunset clause for empowerment initiatives. Though his company was one of the early movers in BEE, banding together with New Africa Investments Limited (Nail) to start MTN, Bekker feared that, if left unchecked, state-enforced empowerment would 'destroy the cohesion of our society'.

He likened it to income tax, which was first introduced in the United Kingdom to finance World War I, but became a permanent feature soon enough. Instead, Bekker wanted BEE to be quick, even if painful. 'Then we put an end to it and build a normal, integrated society where all individuals are treated equally irrespective of race.'[27]

Today, his proposal seems idealistic and overly optimistic. Before the cynicism engendered by the identity politics that would define the latter half of the 2010s, not only in South Africa but across the globe, BEE with a self-destruct mechanism might have been plausible. In 2022, it seems laughable. And imagine a CEO making the same speech in the era of social media. Cancel culture would have made him an instant celebrity for all the wrong reasons.

Nevertheless, analysts regard Naspers's empowerment scheme at Multi-Choice as one of the very best in the field. The initiative at Media24 was less successful, but in a declining industry, that's to be expected.

At a group level, despite not having a formal empowerment initiative, Naspers has probably been the nation's best tool for wealth creation this century. With the Public Investment Corporation, which manages the retirement funds of government employees, as the largest holder of Naspers N-shares, the company has indirectly contributed more than R500 billion to the assets of (mostly black) civil servants. Whether that's enough is an entirely different question.

Creating that much wealth can be exhausting. Especially if you've been at it, first as M-Net MD and later as Naspers CEO, from age thirty-two. '[W]ithin a year after completing business school I had 150 people reporting to me, and I was then chief executive for 22 years without a break,' said Bekker in 2008.

At the time he and his team did a survey of listed media companies and could not find another CEO anywhere in the world who had run a company for that long. This was even before his final five-year contract at Naspers.

'[A]nd every year I had to deliver the financials. And ultimately as the CEO you are responsible for everything – every possible scandal, every possible theft, everything,' he added.[28]

He was in charge to such a degree that he could embark on a year-long sabbatical without worrying that his job would be given to someone else. This was partly because of the management team he had assembled. During Bekker's sabbatical in 2007, Stofberg held the fort.

Bekker would quip that Stofberg was much more sensible than himself. '[W]e've worked together for many years. In several ways he's been an operating chief, so he knows the business from top to bottom. I think he will do particularly well, and the other managers are quite seasoned,' said Bekker in 2006, at the start of his 'gap year'.[29]

And so, before settling in for his final five-year stretch as CEO, Bekker could revisit places such as Norway, where he had done business, but never really experienced as a tourist or as a human being. 'I know the Christiana Hotel and I know the airport and I know the road between them – but I've never been to a fjord, I've never been up a mountain,' he said in 2008, after his return.[30]

Not long before this break, however, Bekker had a wake-up call. He responded by ensuring that anyone who might have a plan to unseat him had more than a fjord to cross or a mountain to climb.

9.

LOCK IN CONTROL

'Koos Bekker – even apart from the preferential potential profit – has become virtually unsackable. He's one of the very best (and richest) publishing executives SA has ever known, but why should he have this added windfall?'

– *FINANCIAL MAIL* EDITORIAL, 2006[1]

'Naspers held on to control as a tightly as a baby baboon to its mother.'   – JANNIE MOUTON[2]

K OOS BEKKER AND PSG FOUNDER JANNIE MOUTON WALKED THE same Stellenbosch streets in the 1960s and 1970s, but their student days did not overlap.

In the early 1970s, Bekker was in Eendrag, a residence of more than 300 male students at the far end of the campus. Cobus Stofberg ('Kango'), his M-Net co-founder, was his senior by one year. The early inhabitants of Eendrag – which had been built in 1961 – joked about digging an underground passage to the university's library. The residence soon developed a reputation for being academically oriented; decades later, other Maties would still poke fun at Eendrag students reputedly sneaking through their fictional tunnel to burn the midnight oil.

Next door to Eendrag is Simonsberg, known less for its academia and more for its parties, the most (in)famous being the annual Simonsberg Metropolitan (the Simon Met) – a dash featuring first-years on horsified broomsticks, and plenty of wine. Affectionately called 'Die Withuis', in part due to its resemblance to the presidential residence in Washington DC, Simonsberg was home to Mouton, who says he lived it up in the late 1960s.[3]

Like Bekker and Stofberg, Mouton would make billions later in life, but before either of them reached that threshold, the Simonsberger would give the two from Eendrag something to think about.

By 2005, PSG, founded by Mouton and Chris Otto in 1994, had established itself as a plucky financial services group. Besides a sprawling network of brokers and clients in its PSG Konsult subsidiary, the company also had a wealth business, and its Stellenbosch office housed a corporate finance team hungry for deals.

'I can't sit around idly. I get bored and then I devise schemes,' Mouton wrote in his memoirs, published in 2011.[4] His scheme, in this instance, involved Naspers.

Mouton knew the company better than most. After all, he had been involved in its listing on the JSE in 1994 when he still headed the brokerage firm Senekal, Mouton and Kitshoff (SMK). There's a front-page picture in *Beeld* to prove it.

Mouton was well aware that, since 1995, Naspers stock came in two varieties – A-shares and N-shares – and that there was a big difference between the two. An A-share carried a thousand votes, but was not traded on the JSE; an N-share carried only one vote, traded freely on the JSE and was entitled to five times the dividend of an A-share.

Sounds complicated, doesn't it? Wouldn't it be nice if there was an infographic to explain Naspers's structure? Maybe even an instructive video with soothing music and friendly executives unpacking how Naspers is controlled by two companies – Keeromstraat 30 Beleggings (Keerom) and Naspers Beleggings (Nasbel) – which together hold enough of the A-shares to wield more than half the votes at shareholder meetings?

By the late 2010s, Naspers had posted exactly such a clip, and the diagrams to go with it, on its website. In 2005, it was still an opaque operation – but Mouton understood it well enough.

'I knew Keerom was a much cheaper way of securing a stake in Naspers,' he wrote. 'Some unlisted shares can be bought at a discount. Therefore one could get a big chunk of Naspers through Keerom or Nasbel, as well as control with high voting rights.'[5]

Even before Naspers went public, Mouton was a keen buyer of the stock. Over the years he had become acquainted with more than a few of the company's long-standing shareholders. And so he noticed that some of the A-shareholders were becoming increasingly disgruntled. Between 2002 and 2005, the value of Naspers's N-shares grew eightfold to more than R100, but the A-shares were unlisted and illiquid.

Many of the shareholders had been invested in Naspers for decades. Ton Vosloo, chief executive when the company went public, later wrote that listing Naspers on the JSE in 1994 was 'probably the biggest empowerment of Afrikaans supporters of all time'.[6]

A decade later, the holders of A-shares weren't feeling all that empowered. Some were getting on in life and had bargained on a steady retirement income. Receiving only a fraction of the dividend was a serious gripe.

Many of them held their stakes indirectly through Keerom or Nasbel, which placed a value of around R2,55 on every A-share. Most of the others had their investments managed by the financial services giant Sanlam. The result: a substantial portion of the voting power in Naspers was in the hands of long-time investors who were not benefiting from the windfall of its investment in Tencent and other successful tech companies.

Those were boom years for the South African economy, with mining, financial, retail and industrial stocks scaling new heights. So, for holders of Naspers A-shares, the contrast was stark.

Mouton's plan was simple: mop up as many of the high-voting shares as possible. He maintained later that he had not tried to gain control of

Naspers, but merely wanted to unlock value for PSG clients, some of whom held A-shares or Keerom stock.

To this end, he pulled together a consortium that included, among others, PSG and empowerment vehicle Arch Equity and made a play for Keerom, which held nearly a third of all the A-shares.

'As a shareholder I knew Keerom was worth much more than the one cent indicated in the results of Nasbel. So we made an offer of 40 cents,' he wrote later. Whether or not this was his intention, the move looked like a corporate raid to some. The Naspers board 'almost went ballistic', he recalled.[7] The consortium later increased the offer to 50 cents a share. Keerom chairman Boetie van Zyl called the PSG bid 'opportunistic'.[8]

On top of this the consortium offered the Keerom board R127 for each Naspers A-share. This was quite a premium, seeing that the directors valued it at only R2,55. And it was a clever move, as it showed Keerom shareholders that there was serious money on the table. (At that time, the company's articles of association gave its board the power to veto any share transfer and to cap the votes of any shareholder at fifty.)

'PSG wants to grab control of the A shares ... It would give them a shareholding that could potentially frustrate the running of the company,' Van Zyl, also a long-serving Naspers director, told Bloomberg in November 2006.[9]

At that time, Bekker was also a director of Keerom. So what were the chances of the company pocketing the lucrative R127 for each A-share? Not good. Bekker had a better idea of what those shares were really worth, and so the directors promptly rejected the PSG offer.

The board also advised shareholders not to accept PSG's bid for their Keeromstraat stock, and instructed Investec to arrange a rival offer to those who wanted to dispose of their holdings.

Meanwhile, Mouton and his consortium held talks with Sanlam CEO Johan van Zyl. Not only did Sanlam manage the portfolios of some of the holders of A-shares; due to historical links with Naspers, the financial services group also held A-shares of its own, and had stakes in both Keeromstraat and Nasbel.

From Naspers's beginning in 1915, its shares were hedged so as to guard against hostile takeovers, Vosloo explains.[10] Back then, this was aimed at protecting the company's political mission. By the time it was listed on the JSE, the structure was retained to help ensure the independence of its media titles.

When Mouton came knocking, Bekker had for a few years been taking punts in parts of the world where foreign investors were often viewed with suspicion. Imagine a South African media company appearing suddenly with a pile of cash, salivating to invest in your company as part of a global shopping spree ...

Here the Naspers control structure came in handy. It could be used to reassure a potential investment's management and other shareholders – perhaps even regulators – that Bekker and his team were a safe bet.

'In several countries where we operate, such as China or India, and in Russia, where we are negotiating, the first question you get asked is, Who are you? And the second is, Can you be taken over?' Bekker said in 2006.[11] And if you are vulnerable to a takeover, 'you get booted out before the second cup of tea'.

A decade earlier, there was no chance of a Naspers executive being denied that second cuppa. Back then, control was neatly tied up because Naspers owned a company named Heemstede Beleggings. Heemstede, in turn, held a 49 per cent stake in Nasbel. And Nasbel owned enough A-shares to cast 45 per cent of the votes in Naspers.[12]

This structure was designed to ensure that Nasbel would not be classified as a company under the control of Naspers – and also, that Nasbel itself would not hold a majority of the votes in Naspers. But with the cooperation of a few minority shareholders, Naspers's board and management would be able to wield the votes in Nasbel. And to exercise control, Nasbel would merely need the support of a few others.

Sounds a bit like when two cousins begin dating after a family reunion, and the parents scramble to prove that the new couple is genetically just far enough removed ...

Keeping votes in the family, so to speak, was part of Naspers's strategy to ensure its independence. But from 1994 onwards the company's other ambitions pulled in a slightly different direction.

Listing on an exchange such as the JSE has distinct benefits. For one, a listed company can raise capital from a deep pool of investors by issuing new shares. Naspers took advantage of this opportunity, tapping the market for funds and issuing more than 200 million new N-shares between 1994 and 2005, swelling its coffers for acquisitions and new ventures.

As a result, however, the combined voting power of the A-shares was diluted. At the time of the PSG consortium's bid, Nasbel no longer carried 45 per cent of the votes in Naspers, but only 34,1 per cent.[13] This made the A-shares held by Keeromstraat hugely significant, as they represented 21,6 per cent of the votes in Naspers. Without Keeromstraat, Naspers's de facto control over Naspers was vulnerable.

That is also why Mouton's discussions with Van Zyl were so important. Between Sanlam and its clients lay another 13,9 per cent of the votes in Naspers, not to mention the stakes in Nasbel and Keeromstraat.

Add Keeromstraat's 21,6 per cent to Sanlam's 13,9 per cent, put it in the hands of a different entity, and suddenly a threshold is crossed. Under South African law, the acquisition of a voting stake of more than 35 per cent triggers a mandatory offer to minority shareholders. In other words, a takeover bid for all of Naspers!

Hard to believe, given that PSG was valued at R1,4 billion and Naspers at more than R40 billion. This was not David taking on Goliath – it was more like David slinging stones at Godzilla, or Jonah trying to swallow the whale.

Whether Mouton and his consortium could have raised the money is anyone's guess. But the proposed deal did expose a crack or two in Naspers's control structure.

And appearances are important – especially when holding more than a third of an awakening giant in a country still speed-dating capitalism and unenthusiastic about democracy. Tencent was strategically important not only in China, but also *to* China. Could an opportunistic bid with no hope of success rattle enough cages in Beijing? Who knows?

Luckily for Naspers, Sanlam's Van Zyl did not only listen to Mouton; he also gave Bekker the opportunity to state his case. And the Naspers CEO gave him 'a very good rationale as to why control was necessary, especially because of the Tencent story', Van Zyl told Ebbe Dommisse.[14]

Van Zyl then took a decision based on the national interest, but also that of Sanlam clients, and approached the A-shareholders about Sanlam taking over their stock and entrenching it in a structure with 'people who get the picture'.[15]

Those people were Bekker and Stofberg. And they certainly got the picture. Those were early days in the life of Tencent, but Bekker and Stofberg must have known that Naspers was on to something really big. At one stage the two held talks with other senior Naspers executives to obtain financial support for the agreement with Sanlam, recalls Vosloo.

But, according to Bekker, what Sanlam wanted for the A-shares, and the Keeromstraat and Nasbel stakes, was too rich for the Naspers directors' blood.[16] So he and Stofberg pulled together and forked out R135 million for half of a company called Wheatfields 221, with Sanlam, represented by Van Zyl, keeping the remaining 50 per cent.

Wheatfields controls 133 350 A-shares, representing some 13 per cent of the voting power in Naspers. As part of the deal, Sanlam agreed not to vote in conflict with Naspers, writes Vosloo. 'No other staff members or directors were approached to invest in the transaction,' he adds.

Was the former chair happy with the outcome? It's hard to tell. Vosloo declined a request to be interviewed for this book, saying he would stick to his memoir. In this he writes that, later in life, he has questions about the future of Wheatfields, as Van Zyl was no longer CEO, and Sanlam's management now dealt with the stake.

'It can be accepted that Bekker and Stofberg will deal with this valuable instrument in the best interests of the company. I am fully satisfied that the matter will be dealt with in such a way that it cements the independence of Naspers,' he writes rather cryptically.[17]

Clearly, Mouton had exposed a hole. Bekker and Stofberg moved decisively to plug it. Remember, the PSG consortium offered R127 per A-share, but Bekker and Stofberg coughed up R1 063,71 per share.

When the Wheatfields transaction became public knowledge, Mouton and his group withdrew their offer for both Keeromstreet and Naspers A-shares, saying their goal had always been to unlock value for shareholders, and they had succeeded.

Asked about the price they had paid to secure 13 per cent of the Naspers voting rights, Bekker said it was 'probably very expensive', but less than the amount Sanlam initially wanted. 'From Sanlam's perspective they got a very good price. And we prevented Naspers from falling into the hands of a raider,' he added.[18]

Sure, a 'raider' would not be able to control Naspers through such a small stake, but it could cause mischief by trying, for example, to block 'special resolutions' for which companies need approval by 75 per cent of those present and voting.

For example, when, in 2019, Naspers sought approval from shareholders to split off Prosus and list the subsidiary on the Euronext stock exchange in Amsterdam, it needed more than 75 per cent of the votes. On that day it received near-unanimous support, but on other occasions, especially when it came to executive remuneration, the outcome tended to be closer.

Both Bekker and Naspers have stressed that control over Naspers does not lie with Wheatfields, but with Nasbel and Keeromstraat, as they have a voting pool and pre-emptive rights between them.

These days, Naspers – of course – fleshes out the structure in a video online. The reason is that Prosus, which is aimed at wooing investors in Europe and beyond, has a control structure similar to that of its parent company Naspers – different classes of shares, with some carrying more votes. In other parts of the world, these convoluted structures are not as common, and need to be explained.

And so, on its website, the company rattles off some nineteen technology and media groups that use differentiated rights and control structures to secure independence, and deter raids and efforts to seize control.

In fact, the A-shares and N-shares played a big role in the decision to list the company in Amsterdam. The Dutch exchange is much friendlier towards these sorts of structures than the major bourses in Britain or the United States, for example.

Though Naspers does not officially regard Wheatfields as part of its control structure, it does provide a safeguard against future attacks.

Hidden deeper in the footnotes of the company's annual reports is the fact that Wheatfields holds not only A-shares, but also a substantial stake in both Nasbel and Keeromstraat. In effect, Bekker and Stofberg found a way to just about control Naspers without this showing up in the control structure. (Why not google 'Naspers Control Structure' and have a look at those diagrams and videos?)

In early 2022, these two varsity mates were both still on the board of Naspers, Bekker as chair. And so they had at least some input into how the company handles its subsidiaries. Remember, Naspers owns 100 per cent of Heemstede, which in turn holds a 49 per cent stake in Nasbel. Bekker and Stofberg have more of a say than most when it comes to deciding how Heemstede votes its 49 per cent stake in Nasbel.

On top of this, Wheatfields owns 168 000 Nasbel shares, enough – with the Heemstede stake – to ensure control of the company that in 2021 still wielded 33,8 per cent of the Naspers voting rights. Wheatfields itself holds more than 12 per cent of the voting rights. This has left a very low threshold for Bekker and Stofberg to whip up among ordinary N-shareholders if Keeromstraat ever falls in the wrong hands.

Bekker did not design the Naspers control structure – he found it that way when he became CEO. But in his first decade at the helm, he sewed up control as tightly as he could. This, of course, helped Naspers to appear more secure when viewed from places such as Brazil, Russia, India and China, where most of its value lies.

Mouton describes it best: 'Nobody who already has an N-share structure, like Naspers, would be keen to relinquish it. They are just sitting
too pretty.'[19]

But even a tight grip on control could fail to save an executive who
disappoints shareholders one time too many. Bekker, however, managed
to survive his failures.

10.

SURVIVE YOUR FAILURES

'Oh, I have made terrible mistakes, lost hundreds of millions of dollars. I doubt many other people in this country have lost more money through stupidity.'

– KOOS BEKKER, 2014[1]

'If he is convinced, he will convince his team and also the controlling boards, regardless of cost.'

– TON VOSLOO, 2018[2]

KOOS BEKKER NEARLY GOT FIRED. NOT ONCE, BUT TWICE. THE first time was in the early days of M-Net, about eighteen months into the business, when he couldn't get the subscriber numbers growing fast enough. '[B]y February 1987, our viewing audience was so pathetic we had to give make-good ads to advertisers on the basis of one-paid, two-free,' he told an interviewer nearly three decades later.[3]

Things were desperate. He even mulled cutting lemon creams from the office coffee supplies,[4] but that would not have been enough to satisfy the real tough cookies: his investors.

'By March our trading results were: turnover of half a million rand, loss of R3,5 million for the month,' he recalled.[5] These sorts of losses were clearly not sustainable, especially as the newspaper groups that had stumped up the capital were also having a tough time with their printed media.

Bekker reckoned his team was a few weeks away from the end, and a 'smell of failure ... was in the air'.[6]

Thanks to the timely arrival of decoders for individual households, sales and subscriber numbers soon picked up, and M-Net broke even the following year. It was hardly a failure; the model just needed time to gain traction. It did, however, have a shaky start – shaky enough to get many a managing director fired.

Luckily for Bekker, he was backed by Ton Vosloo, so he survived. And by the time he took over from Vosloo as Naspers CEO, he was a veteran with international experience. The bigger the stage, though, the bigger the possible failure. Bekker's second close call was the dotcom crash.

After repositioning Naspers to invest in new media opportunities, he piled billions into internet businesses while the dotcom bubble was still inflating. For a while, Naspers, through its international technology subsidiary MIH, swelled along with the bubble, the share price scaling R100 early in 2000. But when sentiment turned against technology stocks, Naspers shares quickly lost their lustre, and declined by nearly 90 per cent over the next two years.

'We were caught with our pants down, and the share price dropped to below R12. For many people, this was a significant part of their investment – it was a disaster. So what do you do? Fire the CEO?' Bekker commented in 2017.[7]

Ironically, while in the throes of this crisis, and with his career hanging in the balance, he was awarded the Sunday Times Top 100 Companies Lifetime Achiever Award. In his acceptance speech, Bekker noted that the media industry came with specific tensions, and that a suitable emblem for it might be a headless chicken. 'People deal with this tension in various ways. Some play golf, some drink, I read myself to sleep on history,' he revealed.[8]

But it's Bekker's belief in historical trends that got him into trouble in the first place. He was well aware of the fact that China had the world's largest economy for most of recorded history, and he believed this nation of more than one billion people would return to that position. Soon after he took the reins at Naspers, he started eyeing China and its emerging internet scene.

'After failing to identify a satisfactory entry vehicle to enter China, Naspers decided to go it alone,' recalls Charles Searle, chief of Naspers's listed internet assets.[9]

In 1998, the company launched the Chinese language portal and internet service provider Maibowang, invested in data-hosting centre 21Vianet, and established portals for finance and sport. But Naspers used technology and systems imported from South Africa, and parachuted people in.

Though Maibowang initially seemed promising, the internet bubble was masking the real state of affairs. In reality, Naspers's expatriate team knew little about the local market, and cost-conscious Chinese consumers shunned Maibowang in favour of cheaper alternatives, adds Searle.[10]

'You know, we went into China, one of the first non-Chinese companies to do so in the media sector. We imported Western managers, and we lost $80 million. We were completely stupid,' Bekker acknowledged in 2008.[11]

And some of his other investments in the Far East, as well as in Europe, the United States and South Africa, were also guzzling cash. As a result, in 2002 he reported the company's first-ever loss. Upon receiving his lifetime achievement award, Bekker told an anecdote about his personal assistant retyping his address list the week before, a task she performed every year. Only this time, half of the Europeans and Americans in the technology, media and telecoms industry were gone – 'bounced, jumped, history'.[12]

But again he survived, probably because he knew what needed to be done. The company announced rapid and drastic adjustments – cost-cutting, scaling back its support for operations that were taking too long to break even, and relentlessly driving each business towards profitability.

'The board never said: "Sell all your unprofitable businesses, close down all your developments, pull the company together." Instead, the board said: "Okay, we understand it's a tough time, we'll back you,"' Bekker recounted.[13]

Nevertheless, he displayed enough intent. He did not renew Hans Hawinkels's contract – this was the person he had sent to Hong Kong to look for a business like Tencent, and who actually found, well, Tencent. Bekker rationalised the portfolio of Chinese investments, holding on only to Tencent in the end. In the United States, he disposed of OpenTV.

'When the internet bubble burst and we were barreling down a slope in 2002, we got the top team together in Bangkok and slashed and burned and restructured, which put us back on the road to profitability,' he recalled later.[14] As a result, the Naspers board and shareholders stuck with him.

Interestingly, one of the assets Bekker got rid of in China turned out to be a unicorn. Founded by Josh Sheng Chen in 1996, 21Vianet had positioned itself as China's first carrier-neutral data centre three years later. At the turn of the century, Naspers acquired a 10 per cent stake in Chen's business. Those were early days for data hosting and managed network services.

If in February 2021 you typed in '21Vianet' on an investment app, you would have found a company on the Nasdaq valued at $7 billion. A year later, however, V-Net (21Vianet's new name) had a market cap of only $1,4 billion. A modest rather than a big miss. And it was the investment in 21Vianet that helped Hawinkels build a relationship with IDG Capital, which later put him on to Tencent.

But there are other opportunities Bekker laments. 'Shares we were offered in Baidu and Alibaba in China, a bigger stake in Facebook, maybe 10 per cent of LinkedIn. It was a lack of either insight or courage,' he told *Rapport*'s Hanlie Retief.[15]

Those are some impressive names. A stake of 10 per cent in LinkedIn would have been worth a bundle today. By 2011, when it listed on the New York Stock Exchange (NYSE), the networking platform sported about 100 million users. Shares rallied more than 100 per cent on the first day, valuing the platform at nearly $9 billion. Five years later, Microsoft bought the company for $26,2 billion. And the number of professionals (and some chancers, obviously) connecting and boasting on LinkedIn has since grown to more than 800 million.

Bekker and his team could have pocketed billions more not only from professional but also from social networking.

Not long after Naspers invested in Mail, the Russian internet business – since renamed VK – took a $200 million punt on Facebook. This was in 2009, when Mark Zuckerberg's company was still privately held and growing user numbers rapidly, but its profitability was far from certain. Mail also held stakes in Groupon – remember when this discount site was all the rage? – and Zynga, developer of the online game FarmVille.

But the Russian company had its own, separate board and Naspers's directors on it were independent, according to Bekker.[16] After Facebook's highly anticipated listing in the United States, Mail sold down its stake in several tranches and pocketed profits of hundreds of millions of dollars.[17]

'Of course, the interesting question is, what is Facebook worth? It started at $100 billion, and dropped to slightly below $50 billion, but it's clearly a vigorous company so it may belt up,' commented Bekker in 2012 after booking a profit from the sale of most of the shares Naspers held through Mail.[18] Nine years later, Facebook was still going strong. The company, renamed Meta Platforms, and by then also the owner of WhatsApp and Instagram, was valued at nearly $900 billion. Mail's original stake of 2,4 per cent would have been worth more than $20 billion.

To be fair, Bekker's Russian investment did well to realise the gains on some of those investments. Around the same time, Mail sold its stakes in what now seems to have been the flavours of the week. Groupon has since lost more than 90 per cent of its value, while Zynga started off with a bang but soon lost momentum and languished below its listing price for nearly a decade, before a modest recovery.

Bekker would have done well to sell out of Mail itself. When, in 2010, the company was listed on the London Stock Exchange (LSE), it was worth considerably more than in early 2022. Shortly after Russia's invasion of Ukraine, and the economic sanctions that followed, Naspers and Prosus wrote down its investment in the company to zero (more in chapter 13).

The really big misses, though, were in China.

Baidu is a Beijing-based search-engine platform – think of it as the Google of China. By 2020 it had a market share of nearly 75 per cent in internet search. In 2010, Bekker described it as 'an excellent local search company ... number one by a fair margin'.[19] That year the platform started using artificial intelligence (AI) to make content discovery on the internet easier, and has since pushed deeper into AI.

By early 2022, Baidu had a market cap of more than $50 billion on the Nasdaq. Ironically, the company's name means 'hundreds of times', which, depending on when Bekker was offered those shares, could be a good indication of the return that was forgone.

When Naspers invested in Tencent, it passed on a few other unicorns. This was because Bekker was set on controlling the businesses he backed. Naspers's pay-TV investment philosophy pervaded its internet approach in China. This limited the opportunities the team in Asia could look at, 'as there were a number of internet businesses where the Group could have acquired a minority interest, but these were turned down,' Hawinkels said in 2018.[20]

By early 2022, Ding Lei (also known as William Ding) was the world's thirty-ninth wealthiest person. And he had made his fortune with an internet gaming company called NetEase.

Online games are big, particularly in China and Japan. That's where NetEase does good business, and after 2015 it also launched fifty mobile games in global markets. But its first success was with the massively multiplayer online role-playing game (MMORPG) Westward Journey Online, which it launched in 2001 when Naspers was still sniffing around China for investment opportunities.

'We had significant discussions about acquiring a stake in NetEase, but we could not get more than 10 per cent,' Hawinkels said in 2021.[21] And no control meant no investment.

Which is strange, because Naspers never had any real control even over Tencent. Sure, it had a say, but foreign holdings in Chinese value-added communications businesses were capped at 50 per cent. Besides, those stakes are held through variable interest entities (VIEs), a rule specific to China which puts extra distance between the investor and the actual company.

Tencent is the market leader in online games, not only in China but globally. And to think Naspers could have had a bite of its closest rival too. NetEase is second in China and in the top seven globally. By early 2022, Ding's company had a market cap of more than $65 billion, and was listed both in Hong Kong and on the Nasdaq.

But NetEase is no Tencent. The only other Chinese company that can be mentioned in the same breath is Alibaba. As Tencent has Pony Ma as its legendary founder, technology conglomerate Alibaba has Jack Ma.

When Jack Ma's company listed in New York in 2014, it was the biggest initial public offering at the time. And Naspers could have had a juicy minority stake in it, something in the region of 7 per cent, according to Hawinkels. Again, this is a tidy sum in a business that was valued at more than $800 billion in 2020.

Add to that the billions Naspers never realised during the dotcom bubble when OpenTV was running hard. Or, on a much smaller scale, the stake Media24 held in South Africa's Curro, but disposed of before the private school group went through its impressive growth spurt.

Do a calculation on the back of a cigarette box, with some loose assumptions, and you'll get to almost $100 billion that Bekker left on the table.

But that's ridiculous. No one who throws spaghetti at a wall is good enough or lucky enough (or both) to see it all stick. And in the early stages, who knows what to pick? Most of the world's greatest investors have stories about the one that got away.

Bekker didn't pick all the winners, because absolutely no one does. Missing out on a good few billion in potential windfalls is hardly a failure.

There were, however, instances on Bekker's watch where Naspers poured in large amounts only to see it evaporate. The $80 million that was lost in China at the start of the tech boom is a good example. Naspers's punts on Chinese pay-TV, web browsing and e-commerce all came to nought before the Tencent investment.

Strangely, Bekker then pushed into a few more traditional media assets – newspapers and magazines. He saw this as an opportunity to apply his company's expertise in various types of content in other emerging markets.[22]

'Several print media acquisitions were chased in Brazil, Argentina, China and India. A few print investments were actually made, and most of those actually lost the group money, severely so in the case of Abril in Brazil,' recalled Searle in 2018.[23]

In 2006, Naspers forked out $422 million for 30 per cent of Abril, a business with assets in TV, book publishing and magazines. By 2014, Bekker and his team had written the value of the investment down to zero, citing headwinds in the Brazilian economy and stronger competition from online competitors.

The losses were four times bigger than during those early years in China, but Bekker was older and wiser. Fat chance of him getting fired this time around. He was no longer a starry-eyed executive trying to convince his board to look east – he was a statesman in the media world, and the company would follow wherever he pointed because *'Koos sê so'.*

If he wanted to buy a turkey in Turkey, he could. And so Naspers did, spending R672 million ($95 million) on an Istanbul-based flash-sale fashion business called Markafoni. In Eastern Europe it bought Fashion Days, a similar outfit, for R435 million, and in Brazil it funded Brandclub with $15 million.[24] This was all between 2010 and 2012. Two years later it raised an impairment charge of more than R1 billion on these three businesses – basically saying that they were worth much less than previously thought. Almost like buying a branded dress in a flash-sale online, only to find that the lulu comes off and you're left with a lemon.

That was a loss in a flash. Some businesses started under Bekker's watch, however, were allowed to limp along for decades. At online retailer Kalahari.com (initially Kalahari.net), for example, profits were scarcer than water in the desert it was named after.

South Africa's high broadband costs held back online shopping. By 2014, according to Oliver Rippel, then senior Naspers executive responsible for Kalahari, it accounted for only 1,3 per cent of consumer goods spend compared with 14 per cent in markets such as the United States and the United Kingdom.[25]

Without scale, South African online retailers could not compete against the country's savvy bricks-and-mortar shopping groups. And Kalahari was even losing ground against newcomer Takealot.com. A bigger threat was looming – foreign giants such as China's Alibaba were eyeing new markets. By 2014, Amazon had already made inroads into South Africa despite not even having a formal presence.

'After many years of losses on Kalahari, and four years on Takealot, we realise we have to work together if we are to survive and prosper,' Rippel stated in 2014 when announcing the merger of the two rivals. Kalahari was no more, as the new entity would trade under the name Takealot.com.

Another half a decade would elapse before the retailer had its first profitable month.[26] And it took the online shopping boom brought about by the Covid-19 pandemic to give the unit enough of a shot in the arm to finally get in the black. 'Takealot.com had its first profitable year,' Naspers announced in its 2021 annual report.

With some businesses, Bekker was prepared to stick it out. Should a succession of losses that eventually swing into profit be seen as a failure? That is debatable.

He had much less patience, though, for some of the traditional media assets in the Naspers stable. Journalists at the newspapers, some of which M-Net was initially established to support, have grim stories about rounds of retrenchment and deep cost-cutting. At the same time, billions were invested and lost in Brazil, not in tech but in print media. In the background, Naspers kept coining it from Tencent.

Bekker survived his failures mostly because they were dwarfed by his successes. Besides the very early years of M-Net, he always had several lines in the water. Some got tangled, others caught minnows, but he did hook at least one whale.

His early backer expresses it best. 'In business, Koos did not hesitate to risk big money in the pursuit of opportunities. This approach has cost Naspers shareholders billions of rands over the years, but earned them billions more,' says Vosloo.[27]

11.

DON'T GET CANED FOR CORPORATE GOVERNANCE

'It sounds wonderful. If you want to be the best soccer team in the world, it's important to wash your hands after using the bathroom. But will you win? Not unless you train the hardest, recruit the best and are merciless in your ambition.' — KOOS BEKKER, 2017[1]

LYFSTRAF (CORPORAL PUNISHMENT) HAD ITS OWN COMPLIANCE regime in the Transvaal of the 1960s. The Laer Volkskool in Heidelberg followed the provincial department of education's rules, and kept records of the floggings administered to naughty boys.

The primary school's *Strafboek* (book of punishment) contains hundreds of entries, with reasons for caning ranging from rudeness and untidiness to throwing stones at passers-by. It also lists the punishments (number of 'strokes') and the names of those flogged.

Good luck with finding Koos Bekker on those pages. It could be that he was an exceptionally well-behaved child. More likely he was just clever enough to follow the rules when he had to. But rules (and laws) differ from guidelines. In business, Bekker's time as the CEO of listed companies coincided with a greater emphasis on sound corporate governance. Ironically, the movement was helped along by the dodgy dealings of another media boss.

The start of the 1990s saw the collapse of a number of publicly traded companies in the United Kingdom, shaking investor confidence and prompting calls for action. In 1991, the accounting profession, the LSE and the Financial Reporting Council appointed a committee to make recommendations that would strengthen corporate governance. Hardly the most exciting of topics – that is, until you add a body floating in the Atlantic Ocean.

British media mogul Robert Maxwell's mysterious death while out on his superyacht and the subsequent revelation that he had misappropriated some £440 million from his companies' pension funds heightened the committee's sense of urgency, and ensured that its work would be closely watched.[2]

Maxwell's yacht was named the *Lady Ghislaine*. Ring a bell? Three decades later, his daughter, Ghislaine, would be convicted for her role in recruiting and grooming teenage girls for the American financier and sexual predator Jeffrey Epstein.[3]

Back in 1992, the committee, chaired by Sir Adrian Cadbury, concerned itself mostly with boardroom abuses. Cadbury, a chocolate tycoon, produced a ninety-page slab of a report. Not the most riveting reading, it dealt with the responsibility of directors, the role of auditors and the relationships among all concerned. The report advocated that 'compliance with a voluntary code, coupled with disclosure, will prove more effective than a statutory code'.[4]

So, no rules but guidelines. Soon, the LSE required listed companies to comply with the Cadbury Code or explain why they weren't. The age of corporate governance had begun.

The United Kingdom might have had its swindlers at that time, but at the southern tip of Africa there were also some real *skelms* (crooks). More than 20 000 investors were left stranded when it became clear that some of the seaside stands Masterbond had been punting as part of its property portfolio were actually *in* the sea. By the time the company went into liquidation in 1991, more than R600 million had been raised from investors who were promised annual returns of up to 20 per cent.[5]

'I saw what happened in boardrooms at that time; the board meeting lasted an hour, it was quite collegial, and governance was light,' Bekker told the *Financial Mail* in 2017.[6] Of course, he had not been involved in Masterbond, but was referring to M-Net which had listed on the JSE in the same year that Masterbond was picked apart.

To counteract the chumminess of boardrooms, the Institute of Directors South Africa (IoDSA) established a committee chaired by retired judge Mervyn King to examine corporate governance and formulate a set of guidelines. Earlier King himself had also dabbled in business and in the mid-1980s ran Tradegro, a retail group with Checkers, Russells and Dion in its stable.

The retired judge clearly decided he would not be outdone by Cadbury. When published in 1994, the King Report on Corporate Governance was recognised internationally as the 'most comprehensive publication on the subject embracing the inclusive approach to corporate governance', according to the IoDSA.[7] Yawn-worthy stuff.

More excitingly, the scandals kept coming. Later in the 1990s, Health & Racquet Club owner LeisureNet collapsed under a mountain of debt, booking two of the company bosses a few years behind bars for fraud. At the urging of then president Nelson Mandela, British billionaire Richard Branson bought the assets and it became the bulk of his Virgin Active business.[8]

LeisureNet is a decent enough example of cooking the books with a South African flavour. But in the United States, Enron perfected the recipe. When the American energy company imploded in 2001, destroying $60 billion in shareholder value, it took its auditor down with it. At the time, Arthur Andersen was one of the 'big five' auditing firms, but after the reckoning there was only a 'big four'.

At Enron, the executives, directors and auditors did not do their jobs properly, and cosy relationships and blurred lines between accounting and consulting resulted in large-scale fraud and a financial disaster. In the wake of the scandal, corporate governance measures went into overdrive.

The US Congress swiftly passed the Sarbanes-Oxley Act that made it a criminal offence for CEOs and CFOs to sign off misleading financial statements. By making it a crime to retaliate against whistle-blowers, the legislation also aimed to protect those who uncover fraud in companies.

What happened in the United States mattered to Bekker as well. Even before the Enron bomb went off, subsidiaries MIH and OpenTV were listed on the Nasdaq, and in 2002 Naspers itself took a secondary listing on the technology-heavy bourse. This was quite the event for the company. When, around that time, the top floor of the Cape Town headquarters was turned into a posh function venue, it was christened the 'Nasdak' (Nas-roof).

The listing on the real Nasdaq meant that Bekker and Naspers CFO Steve Pacak had to certify that the reports they signed off complied with the new law, and were a true reflection of the company's financials.

In 2002, King produced the King II Report, to which Naspers duly committed itself.

Bekker, of course, retained the independent perspective of a sceptic. After his first sabbatical in 2007, during which he quietly sold a substantial chunk of his Naspers stock, he touched on corporate governance in a TV interview. Markets were most efficient when information was available to all participants and people couldn't do shady deals and manipulate share prices, he said.

'On the other hand, corporate governance is a bit of a fad at the moment, and some elements clearly go too far. So in corporate dealings the fact that you disclose is neither here nor there,' he argued.[9]

This was before it became public knowledge that he had sold those shares while on sabbatical. So it was quite a cheeky comment, especially when he continued: 'I think it's the way the information is treated. If every profit by every chief executive is regarded as a great robbery, then clearly the free market system is undermined.'

Giving kudos to another giant of South African business who had been catching flak for taking home more than R50 million the previous year, he added: 'but if people are fairly mature and say, well, Whitey Basson is an excellent retail manager, he ought to make a living, and grant him that when he cashes in, I think it's fine'.[10]

But the *zeitgeist* was turning against congratulating business people for making money. The advent of social media helped disgruntled groups the world over to organise petitions and protests against society's so-called one per cent – those viewed as rich or privileged or somehow getting a free ride, while the 99 per cent struggle to make ends meet.

This sentiment gave rise to movements such as Occupy Wall Street and was quickly latched on to by left-leaning political factions such as the Economic Freedom Fighters (EFF) and, later, the 'Radical Economic Trans-formation' wing of the ANC.

In a society as unequal as South Africa, white men in their sixties raking in billions became a source of both intense fascination and severe criticism, spawning a number of best-selling books and pushing loaded tags such as 'white monopoly capital' and 'Stellenbosch Mafia' into the public discourse.

Bekker made his 'great robbery' comment at the start of his last stint as CEO. It was just before the release of yet another report on corporate governance – King III – and only a year before Jacob Zuma would accede to the presidency.

Though the decade that followed brought Bekker and other Naspers shareholders fabulous gains, it was a sad one for South Africa. Not only did it bring economic stagnation, and widen the gap between rich and poor; the last years of Zuma's tenure in the Union Buildings also carried the stench of dysfunction and corruption.

The president's allegedly dodgy ties with the Gupta family were investigated left, right and centre (both politically and journalistically). But Zuma and his friends had their defenders too. The Gupta family conveniently owned *The New Age*, a daily paper, and ANN7, a news channel on DStv.

ANN7 was something to behold. The channel was a potent cocktail of activism, sensationalism and bad grammar served up as journalism – evangelically pro-Zuma, vehemently anti-anyone who opposed Zuma.

DStv, of course, belonged to Naspers's MultiChoice. By late 2017, the calls to pull the plug on ANN7 could no longer be ignored, and Bekker spoke up.

'So we've debated removing the channel. For example, you can just say, I'm taking you off air, I'm abandoning the contract. So we've debated, but we really don't think in a democratic, open country it's a good idea,' he told Moneyweb in 2017.[11]

Around the same time, Bekker traded verbal blows with former communications minister Yunus Carrim, who implied that Naspers had leaned on the government to influence his department's policy on digital encryption.

This was shortly after Jacques Pauw had released his damning book *The President's Keepers*,[12] and a stream of investigative reports about Zuma's government appeared in *Daily Maverick*, News24 and *Sunday Times* under the banner #GuptaLeaks. It painted a picture of business people, such as the Gupta family, holding sway over ministerial appointments and government policy.

Carrim, who served in one of Zuma's frequently reshuffled cabinets for less than a year, pointed to a meeting with Bekker in 2013, not long after he was appointed minister. The public broadcaster's migration to digital transmissions had been dragging along for years, and there was hope that a new political head would get it to move quicker.

Asked at the time whether he had engaged with Carrim, Bekker said, 'not that intensively', and that he would like to do so. 'Clearly he needs to set down a policy for digital migration that makes sense, and see it through. It's not a very difficult thing to do, so many countries have already completed it.'

The minister did not enjoy their encounter. In a 2017 *Financial Mail* interview, he called the Naspers boss 'astonishingly arrogant', and added: 'He was dogmatic, rigid and pushy. He seemed annoyed with me for not seeing how brilliant he is. Brilliant he may be, but that doesn't give him the right to his culture of entitlement.'[13]

Not long before the meeting, MultiChoice concluded a R533 million transaction with the SABC that would give the pay-TV platform access to the state broadcaster's extensive archives. As part of the deal, the SABC would be allowed to air a 24-hour news channel as well as an entertainment channel on DStv.[14] Separately, ANN7 also got a channel on the network, and received several payments from MultiChoice over the following five years totalling more than R200 million.[15]

When Bekker's meeting with Carrim took place, he was still Naspers CEO, and MultiChoice represented a significant portion of its parent company's cash flow and profit. The suggestion by Carrim that Bekker had once met with him regarding encryption was perfectly accurate, Naspers said in a statement in December 2017. 'Here are the facts: this meeting took place in Pretoria and was for the full duration also attended by Minister Pravin Gordhan, whom we greatly respect. Gordhan can attest to the content of the meeting and whether any Gupta-related or any other illegal matter was discussed.'

But the pundits were not convinced, and barrels of ink were expended in editorials and think-pieces decrying the allegedly inappropriate behaviour of Bekker, MultiChoice and Naspers. Why, it was asked, were they so happy to sign deals worth hundreds of millions of rand with both the state broadcaster and a channel so closely linked to the controversial family?

No wonder cartoonist Zapiro that week drew Bekker with both his hands stuck in cookie jars labelled 'Influence Peddling' and 'Gupta Greasing'. On a wall behind the Naspers boss was the MultiChoice logo, its tagline reading 'enriching lies' instead of 'enriching lives'.

The company denied any wrongdoing, shot down some of the allegations, and promised to investigate others. With operations in 120 countries, Naspers was happy to leave it up to the MultiChoice board to conduct a probe, and said it had confidence in this company handling the matter following its governance procedures. The findings of the investigation were announced early in 2018 with the pay-TV business's CEO Calvo

Mawela admitting that some 'mistakes' had been made, but that there was no evidence of corruption. The full report was not released to the public as MultiChoice said it contained commercially sensitive information. ANN7, however, got the chop – MultiChoice did not renew the channel's contract.[16]

'If Naspers reacts recklessly, and takes away the autonomy of a local, fully constituted board, it's very serious stuff. Where does it end? Next time it will be Brazil and the time after that, Greece,' Bekker told an interviewer in 2017.[17]

He likened the issue with ANN7 to famous actors distancing themselves from controversial movie boss (and later convicted sex offender) Harvey Weinstein. 'Meryl Streep is seen with him in a photo that was taken five years ago, when she still thought he was great. In the meantime the scandals have been revealed, and now it is an embarrassment to her. That's more or less MultiChoice's position. What was initially broadcast was okay, but today it is an embarrassment,' Bekker added.[18]

Naspers also made sure to state that it was not dinner mates (or bedfellows) with those accused of capturing the South African state. 'For the record, neither of Ton Vosloo, previous chair of Naspers, Koos Bekker, present chair, or Bob van Dijk, CEO, had to their best recollection ever in any country met any member of the Gupta family at any but public functions, never discussed anything with them, never even received written communications or a single telephone call from them,' the Naspers board said in a statement.

Politics is an ugly business. Bekker has often shrugged it off as part of the job if you work in the media. But at that time, the tension in South Africa was palpable. In the weeks leading up to the ANC's elective conference at Nasrec to choose the ruling party's new leader, investors were holding their breath. It looked far from certain that Cyril Ramaphosa, generally viewed as more business friendly than his rival Nkosazana Dlamini-Zuma, would win the battle.

Bekker had a battle of his own at the Naspers annual shareholder meeting a few months earlier. And he really put his foot in it. Have another look at the snarky quote at the beginning of this chapter, the one about corporate governance sounding 'wonderful' but being like a professional soccer team washing their hands after visiting the loo.

'Once you have won, then you can look at things. If you lose, the best governance in the world can't help you,' said Bekker in the same breath.[19]

And remember the earlier comment about board meetings in the 1990s lasting less than an hour? A quarter of a century later, it was a different story. Meetings went on forever, hardly anyone read the annual report, and rules were written by accountants who'd never run a business in their lives, Bekker complained.[20]

After two initial hiccups, investors were mostly impressed by Bekker's performance as CEO, which brought with it the incredible wealth creation of the Tencent investment.

But when, in 2015, he moved into the chairman's position, they did start taking a real interest in the pay package of his successor. Van Dijk's growing pile of Naspers share options and the murky set of incentives listed in the company's annual report were causes for concern. And so, the Naspers annual general meeting two years later was billed as a show-down between some shareholders, such as asset manager Allan Gray, and the Naspers board over executive remuneration. In the end it will be remembered for Bekker silencing activist shareholder Theo Botha, who came armed with a single Naspers share.

Botha, who has been an uncomfortable presence at many share-holder meetings, had a string of questions about Van Dijk's pay package. The CEO, he contended, derived great benefit from Tencent even though the investment was made long before his appointment and with Naspers's management having a very limited influence over the Chinese com-pany's performance.[21]

The discount between the Naspers share price and the value of its stake in Tencent had widened from 2014 to 2017 (and would widen even further in the next half a decade), causing unhappiness among share-holders.

Naspers management was essentially continuing with Bekker's e-com-merce investment strategy, piling billions into businesses that were years away from showing a profit. In the meantime, Van Dijk was earning a tidy sum, mostly in share options, as the Tencent share price kept rising, dragging Naspers along with it. Botha was outraged that the CEO scored fifty out of fifty for 'group financial results' in his annual performance-related incentive outcomes despite presiding over a largely loss-making portfolio.[22]

When Botha wanted to ask more questions about this and employee share-incentive trusts, Bekker suggested that he and those with further concerns speak to lower-ranking company officials afterwards, and shut him down. 'I've ruled. That's the end of it,' Bekker declared.[23]

No surprise then that half of the N-shareholders voted against the remuneration policy, but the high-voting A-shares – most of which were held by entities in which either Naspers itself or Bekker and his long-time mate Cobus Stofberg had a big say – ensured that it passed.

Equivocating about corporate governance was a mistake. Whether Bekker in practice flouts or follows King's guidelines is not the issue; his remarks were irresponsible. Likening it to a hand-washing exercise emitted a frequency that perked up the ears of every corporate governance hound in the country.

The editorial response, from most publications outside the Naspers fold, was basically an industry saying 'sies, man'. Meanwhile, the ANN7 issue was brewing in the background.

Bekker even got rapped on the knuckles by none other than the King of corporate governance. 'I'm afraid I don't agree with Mr Bekker,' said King in an interview with Power FM's Andile Khumalo.[24] His fourth report had been published just the previous year.

'If you do an analysis of Naspers, you will see that the majority of its share value from a monetary point of view is made up from its offshore investment in Tencent. Its local businesses are not performing as well as Tencent. So the question arises – if, let's say, tomorrow it's discovered that Tencent in its supply chain is using child labour, what will happen is that there will be a huge diminution in the value of Tencent overnight,' King explained. Child labour, ouch.

Treating corporate governance as a nice-to-have and focusing only on financial gain was actually yesterday's thinking, he said. 'The question of being a responsible corporate citizen is absolutely essential for the collective mind of the board to ensure the company retains value.'

But even in the good times, without King's fictional child labour scandal, the total value of Naspers's holding in Tencent was not passed through to shareholders – the company simply was not willing to transfer the full Tencent dividend. But in the years that followed, it gradually disclosed more details of its unlisted e-commerce assets to the public.

According to Naspers, listing Prosus on the Euronext in Amsterdam in 2019 was a major step towards addressing the discount. The results were not instantaneous; in fact, the discount grew further.

In 2021, Prosus and Naspers came up with a share swop scheme that it hoped would unlock value. Again, investors did not exactly reach for their vuvuzelas. In an unprecedented move, a group of thirty-six asset managers actually drafted a letter to Bekker, expressing their dissatisfaction at the intricate deal.

'We believe that this complex transaction, while described by management as the "best solution" on the table, results in what we believe are worsening governance outcomes which will do very little to reduce the substantial discounts within [Naspers] and [Prosus] and could even widen them,' wrote the group, which together held R3,6 trillion in assets under management.

Again, executive remuneration was a serious concern. 'We believe proceeding with this transaction in its current form despite the express reservations of such a large contingent of shareholders would significantly undermine [Naspers] and [Prosus] governance undertakings,' the asset managers added.

Between the initial announcement of the planned deal and the shareholder vote, the company disclosed estimates of the value of its unlisted e-commerce businesses, and tweaked the proposed CEO and CFO remuneration structures to align them more directly to performance.

But, again, the decision was a foregone conclusion. Thanks to the high-voting A-shares, Naspers and Prosus both passed the shareholder resolutions, and the deal went ahead. And so, through a cross-holding agreement, Prosus came to hold 49 per cent of Naspers, and Naspers 56,92 per cent of Prosus.[25]

Part of the problem investors and commentators had with Naspers was that it just seemed too good to be true. Add to that the convoluted Naspers control structure and the perception that Bekker and Stofberg pulled the strings, and it's not hard to see why some shareholders felt neutered.

Just months after Bekker's spat with Botha, Steinhoff International would be added to the South African roll of corporate dishonour. Steinhoff, where a mountain of undisclosed debt was uncovered after the abrupt departure of long-time CEO Markus Jooste, had some of the nation's most esteemed directors.

Naspers itself had a good crop of board members. In his memoir, Vosloo lists many of them, and then says: 'With individuals of that calibre at your side, you do not need Cadbury or King corporate governance prescriptions to lead a business successfully.'[26]

For Bekker too it was more about the underlying business. As far as he knew, he told the *Financial Mail* in 2017, tech companies did not fail due to governance. 'That's not where the failure in tech occurs. It occurs when you misread the consumer, when your tech gets behind, when you lose a top engineer.'[27]

This may be so. But publicly traded firms that slip up on corporate governance also tend to get caned more severely than any schoolboy in the 1960s.

12.

PUBLICITY IS YOUR FRENEMY

'Unscrambling the low-profile Bekker is about as impossible as unscrambling M-Net's pattern without a decoder.'
— *FINANCIAL MAIL*, 1986[1]

'I'm in the lucky position that I can still go out to buy a loaf of bread and no one knows who I am.'
— KOOS BEKKER, ABOUT THIS BOOK, 2020

WHERE BETTER TO ESCAPE JOHANNESBURG'S HUSTLE AND bustle than next to the Indian Ocean? No need for electricity, just a wooden bungalow near Plettenberg Bay, with gas for cooking and a paraffin fridge to keep things cool. This must have been Koos Bekker's thinking when he rented a holiday home at Keurboomstrand early in 1988.

Though Bekker could not have been sure, he must have had an inkling that it would be the year M-Net would reach its break-even number of 150 000 subscribers. An important threshold for this man in his mid-thirties, as it would trigger a big payday.

There was reason to be optimistic about life, and so, on a Monday afternoon in January, he and his wife, Karen, went to lunch in Plett, leaving son Niel and daughter Cato in the care of a domestic worker.

Imagine the horror when, after a good meal, they returned to find the house had burnt down. Thankfully, Alan Read, a former rugby player, was in the vicinity when the wooden structure caught fire. A decade and a half earlier he had scored a memorable try for Western Province in an 8–17 loss against the British Lions.[2] In 1974 his efforts were in vain, but on this occasion he saved the day.

Responding to a cry for help, Read got to the burning house when 'everyone was safe except the baby girl who was sleeping in the lounge,' he told a reporter.[3]

The former winger rushed into the burning building and brought the two-month-old Cato to safety. He then called the fire brigade, but by the time the men with the ladders and hoses arrived, the structure was beyond rescue. Bekker and his wife arrived half an hour later. A tragedy had been avoided.

The story reveals something interesting. Firstly, in the eyes of the reporter, Read seemed to have been the bigger celebrity. After all, he had played for 'Province'. By 1988 M-Net was still a newbie in Cape Town, and had yet to be launched on the Garden Route.

Secondly, Read seems to have been the reporter's only source. There was no comment from the Bekkers. The couple was even referred to as 'Cobus' and 'Karin', a further indication that the journalist probably did not even have the opportunity to take their names down in person.

'Koos prefers to fly under the radar', or 'he doesn't like publicity', or 'does Koos know about it?' were some of the responses from former colleagues and old acquaintances in the course of rejecting requests for interviews for this book.

Bekker is a man who guards his personal life closely, says Ton Vosloo.[4] And the blaze in Keurbooms is a good example of how, when it comes to family affairs, Bekker restricts public access. But is he a media-shy media boss?

Well, he is hardly a recluse. Visitors to Babylonstoren, the farm near Paarl that he and Karen bought in 2007 and have redeveloped into a world-class attraction, may spot him pruning a tree somewhere on the eight acres of cultivated gardens. (Disgruntled former hacks might quip that he's been trimming and cutting newspaper budgets for decades.)

Bekker also has impressive homes in Cape Town and Amsterdam. In 2013, he added a stately manor in the Cotswolds, some 200 kilometres southeast of London, to his property portfolio. Actor Johnny Depp was rumoured to also have been interested, but the South African billionaire scooped up Hadspen House and rejigged it into The Newt, a luxury destination that is the stuff of high-end lifestyle magazines.[5]

Type his name (Bekker's, not Depp's) on YouTube, and more than fifty interviews pop up. Mostly dressed in a blue or grey shirt, often dry-mouthed, he discusses anything from social media trends to Nelson Mandela's legacy to the gherkin-eating habits of ladies in Sea Point. And obviously Naspers's financial results. There is an entertaining video of an address to MBA students in the Netherlands, and an awkward clip of him presenting the interviewer with a flower crown while marketing a garden day at Babylonstoren.

In all those hours of footage, however, he volunteers very little about his personal life. When asked directly about family and his upbringing, he usually segues into another topic. He seems content to make general statements, such as 'I grew up on a mealie farm, quite primitive', but will not divulge anything about the relationships between family members, whether they were role models, or any of the titbits an unguarded interviewee would usually share.

Likewise, Bekker declined to be interviewed for this book, or provide the author with any other form of assistance, saying he had known many people over the years who had become rich and famous, but it had never done them much good. Not that this book would make him famous; he already is. Still, he believes that anything he does to aid such a project would go against his principles.

'People in the business of entertainment have to remember they're just the stage manager, not the star attraction,' Bekker told an interviewer in 1986.[6] And he seems to have followed the same line ever since.

He has certainly not expended the same energy building a business celebrity brand as, say, Tesla CEO Elon Musk. Imagine Bekker hosting NBC's *Saturday Night Live* or doing the 'Walk like an Egyptian' on stage while launching a bakkie that resembles an ashtray. And would he tweet that his company's share price is too high? Would he tweet at all?

Though the handle @KoosBekker is on Twitter, it doesn't have a blue tick next to it – that all-important mark of official verification – and at the time of writing it was completely inactive. Compare that to Johann Rupert, Bekker's former business partner in NetHold, who tweets as @cutmaker and had nearly 24 000 followers by early 2022. Or former First National Bank CEO Michael Jordaan, who sported more than 220 000.

Musk, who is probably an extreme example, has sent more than 18 000 of those short updates to the world, and boasts some 100 million followers.

And don't even bother looking for Bekker on LinkedIn. You'll find his cousin – also Koos Bekker – who is the CEO of South Ocean Holdings, a manufacturer of low-voltage cables.

None of this necessarily means that Bekker is scared of publicity. He might not say much about his family, but they don't exactly hide in the shadows either. His wife, son and daughter have public profiles that are quite independent of the media mogul's.

Karen was one of the first faces on South African television. As an SABC presenter from 1976 onwards, she entered living rooms when TV was still such a novelty that the newspapers reported on the entire evening's programming the next day.

'Last night one got the impression that things were amuck behind the scenes, unnerving the announcers. Karen Roos could not say anything right, and Michael de Morgan appeared ruffled,' read a snippet in the *Rand Daily Mail* one Thursday of that year.[7]

In New York, while Koos was studying at Columbia, Karen continued her career in the magazine industry, working for *Glamour,* and upon their return to South Africa she was fashion editor of *Cosmopolitan*. In 1990, with the backing of Naspers, she launched a high-end title called *Red*. The magazine hit the shelves just as a recession hit consumers and did not last long, but it was a high-profile project. Roos was even on the judging panel of the Miss South Africa pageant that year.

In the 1980s and 1990s, the *Sunday Times* often listed her as one of South Africa's Best-Dressed Women, and she walked away with the honours in 1998. More recently she has been lauded as a decorating icon, and she has published a number of books on the topic.

Though Bekker has quipped that Karen says she 'doesn't do wife',[8] he told a room full of MBA graduates in 2014: 'It's very important who you marry,' adding with a chuckle, 'so watch out!'[9] In the same speech, extolling the work ethic of China, he said that he wasn't about to push his children as hard as Chinese mothers do.

Cato has worked in radio and television. In 2020 she started producing and presenting a reality show called *Die Uitnodiging* (The Invitation) that aims to reconcile estranged family members or friends on one of DStv's Afrikaans channels, Via.

Niel started as an entertainment journalist but has since built a name as a photographer using film. In 2015 he co-founded a co-working space in Cape Town. His partner, Lucie de Moyencourt, is an artist and illustrator, with more than 40 000 followers on Instagram.

None of the Bekkers are off the grid, but they seem to have a similar approach when it comes to sharing details online or with the media.

Good luck trying to find Bekker saying anything about his father, who finished his career in the upper echelon of the apartheid state's security establishment. Cor Bekker had studied Afrikaans and Latin at university, became a teacher and schoolmaster, and then a lecturer at a teachers' training college in Heidelberg. Thereafter he became the first civilian to be enlisted in the Bureau for State Security (BOSS), and had 'an enormous influence on the products we delivered', writes former colleague PC Swanepoel in his self-published memoir *Really Inside BOSS*.

'When he retired on pension he was the Deputy Director-General and known throughout the civil service because of his chairmanship of a host of interdepartmental committees,' adds Swanepoel.[10]

Another former colleague, Maritz Spaarwater, describes the elder Bekker as an excellent academic, and one of two very powerful men who supported the National Intelligence Service's young director-general, Dr Niël Barnard.[11]

Barnard would go on to play an important behind-the-scenes role in South Africa's transition from minority rule to multiparty democracy. In his memoir, he published a picture of Cor and Deleen Bekker, Koos's parents, in Rio de Janeiro. He identified Bekker merely as a senior colleague.[12] Had the junior Bekker been more open to publicity, this titbit would probably have been tweeted, retweeted and debated.

While Ton Vosloo gets most of the credit for the political footwork in securing M-Net's broadcasting licence in the 1980s, having a father with a good reputation in the civil service surely would not have harmed Bekker's chances of launching pay-TV.

Despite being thrifty with personal information, Bekker has done a masterful job in building his profile. It is not clear whether this public image came into being by design or by accident, but judging by the strategic nature and careful planning in some of his other endeavours, chances are that Bekker read the mood and capitalised on it from the very start.

When one examines the more than three decades' worth of source material, two themes emerge: Koos the doer (or problem-solver) and Koos the thinker (or opinionista).

Early in 1987, the *Sunday Times* compiled a list of the people South Africa would be talking about that year. It tapped Bekker as the most likely to change the face of television, as he was expected to launch a massive drive for viewership and not, like the state broadcaster, for National Party membership.

'While the SABC broadcasts lurid displays of political sloganeering, M-Net will broadcast sexy adult movies, interspersed with rock 'n roll,' predicted the newspaper.[13] The problem Bekker had to solve for South Africa was how to make TV entertaining.

Though his stated intention was to remain behind the scenes, the press soon started quoting the pay-TV founder and used him as a counterpoint in stories about the loss-making state broadcaster. And when the

SABC started criticising M-Net's programming plans as too risqué, Bekker's response positioned him to seem much cooler than the prudish establishment in Auckland Park.

An M-Net decoder became a status symbol. And suddenly there was a new divide, this time not along racial lines, but based on whether the picture on a household's tube started blurring and jiggling at the end of Open Time.

Bekker benefitted by association. He was the entertainment guru, the bringer of magic who emancipated families with recent American movies, international sport and trendy toons for the kids. And by placing presenters of different races in the same frame, he beamed the first visible signs of a changing South Africa to the screens of thousands, then hundreds of thousands and then millions of viewers.

M-Net took off. By late 1988, the channel started breaking even on a monthly basis, not even half a decade after it had been conceptualised.[14] The company listed on the JSE and became a stand-out success on the bourse at a time when a deep recession was battering most other stocks.

With broadcasting being such a political game, both locally and internationally, Bekker was forced to build up a strong network of contacts. Just think of the constant negotiations with the authorities about licences and regulation. As a thirty-something he already interacted with bigwigs in different disciplines and, as he expanded the pay-TV business abroad, in several countries.

'Pay television is very interesting, the problems it poses with technology, people, regulation, politics. You know when you open up your inbox in the morning, you often say, "oh God, there goes the business!"' he joked in 2014.[15]

Back in the 1980s and 1990s Bekker got massive kudos from the business community for making a success of such a gutsy venture. When Johann Rupert, fresh back from London, felt that he'd struggle to live in a country without cellphones, he first approached Bekker to see if they could start a mobile operator. Though Rupert eventually invested in Vodacom, it shows how highly Bekker was regarded.

At the turn of the century, he was the wunderkind roped in to help present the bid for the 2006 FIFA World Cup.[16] South Africa narrowly missed out, but four years later he was again part of a star-studded cast of statesmen, politicians and business leaders who flew to Zurich to convince FIFA that 2010 should be Africa's turn. With the bid a success, he was chosen to be on the local organising committee.

A week after the final in which Spain beat the Netherlands 1–0 in Johannesburg, Bekker described the tournament as a lever that shifted people's perceptions.

'In the past, emerging nations would have been allowed to join the lads in kicking the ball around on the grass, but the brains who pulled the strings up there in the stadium would have been from Europe. Last Sunday at Soccer City, the physical work down on the field was being done by Dutch and Spanish labour, while the organisers in the suites were, what, South Africans?!' he wrote in a newspaper column.[17]

And in the euphoria of hosting the event, an optimist could be forgiven for hoping it would solve the ultimate South African problem – binding the nation together by organising something spectacular.

The quip about Dutch and Spanish labour is a classic example of Bekker's off-beat writing style, and formed part of an opinion piece written for *City Press*. This particular Sunday paper is, of course, owned by Media24, a subsidiary of Naspers.

Since taking the reins at Naspers in 1997, Bekker has written more than a dozen contributions to the publications in his stable. He sticks to opinion pieces, and they all carry a disclaimer that he is writing in his personal capacity.

This particular piece was entitled 'Overcoming the victim mentality', and argued that, after hosting a successful World Cup, South Africa should finally realise it deserved a seat at the global table. His reasoning linked up to some of his public appearances around the same time. At the Global Forum 2010 he said that foreign aid engendered corruption, and went as far as declaring that Africa should stop accepting alms from richer nations.

'You know, all the foreign aid of all the countries together is $120 billion. The world total global trade is $12 trillion. It is 1 per cent of world trade. It's peanuts. So if you are going to be a prostitute, at least sell for a decent price!' he said in a panel discussion.[18]

Shooting from the hip about global issues doesn't sound like part of the job description for a CEO and later board chair, does it? Yet Bekker often takes aim and pulls the trigger, probably hoping to leave his mark on other parts of society. And his informed style and rhetoric displays a sense of careful and strategic planning, writes Dr Gabriël Botma, media studies lecturer at Stellenbosch University.[19] As an example, Bekker would float his ideas on the position of the Afrikaans language and culture in Afrikaans newspapers, while publishing his musings on diversity, nation-building and broader political issues in the English media.

In an academic article entitled 'Koos says ...: A critical discourse analysis of the meta-capital of a prominent South African media tycoon', Botma identifies several themes with which Bekker goes outside his remit as company boss.

In Bekker's above-mentioned piece on the World Cup, the M-Net founder styles himself as a critical patriot, and the theme of African and South African optimism is at its peak in 2010, according to Botma.

Judging by the cynical tone of a more recent contribution to News24, with South Africa battling through the harsh restrictions of the Covid-19 pandemic, Bekker's optimism was dampened by the intervening decade of government failure and corruption and the looming threat of asset expropriation.

'So when the first mortgaged field of the scruffy farmer in the two-tone shirt gets confiscated without compensation, the last international investor will zip through customs at OR Tambo International Airport,' he wrote.[20] Still a critical patriot, but leaning more towards the critical than the patriotic side.

Some of the other themes Botma sees Bekker pushing into the public discourse are Darwinian evolution theory, the position of Afrikaans in education, the behaviour of Afrikaners, and an open-minded look at the rise of China.

The mogul seems to use informal language to disarm the reader. In the Covid piece he refers to himself as a 'mampara' (that's South African for numbskull). Botma spots a seeming nonchalance in Bekker's writing. And that certainly is not new. Back in the 1970s when Bekker edited the student newspaper *Die Matie*, his writing displayed similar traits. Even a school essay fits the bill.

This informal, casual approach has allowed Bekker to package some powerful ideas, whether you agree with them or not, in an almost non-threatening way. In the process he's been able to criticise, for example, the ruling party's policy of 'cadre deployment' – basically parachuting ANC members into important public sector positions based on loyalty rather than skill – without taking much personal flak in public or putting his company in the firing line. This was, of course, before the ANN7 saga mentioned earlier.

And his opinion pieces are probably published just as they've been written. According to Botma, it is not only unlikely that editors at Naspers publications would reject a Bekker piece, he also probably had a say in the extent to which it should be edited, and how it should be presented. This would also reduce the chances of changing whatever he wanted to say.

So if you read something written by Koos Bekker in a Media24/Naspers title, it's probably still in its original form. It reveals not only how influential a boss he is, but also how high his quality of writing and expression is. A journalist with the grit to make it all the way to editor would likely never publish an article she or he is not allowed to panel-beat if that piece is not up to standard. And a high standard at that.

Publicity seems to be neither Bekker's enemy nor his friend. But his approach is to use it in a very targeted way. His fame is not of the fluffy, celebrity sort. Spending habits or glamorous parts of his lifestyle get no airplay.

His profile is a serious one. He has built a reputation for getting tough things done. And when he airs those opinions of his, there is hardly any noise from his personal life, so his message comes across loud and clear.

Then there is his day job. In the field of communication, Bekker is world-renowned. His reputation is so good that his successor as CEO travelled some distance for a quick first meeting with Bekker in London. This was in 2010, years before Bob van Dijk joined Naspers.

'I was living in the Bay Area close to San Francisco at the time, and I flew in for a one-hour meeting. I spent 22 hours on the plane just to meet him, but it was a good meeting,' he recalls.[21]

13.

DANCE WITH
THE DEVIL

'When I was a kid, the future of South Africa looked abysmal. As a student looking ahead at my life, I expected civil war, claustrophobia, agitators baying for Stalinism, police shooting civilians – a torn society. And on a personal level, as a white South African, I expected to be despised wherever I went in the world.'

– KOOS BEKKER, 2006[1]

'When an industry is young and small, society generally regulates it very lightly. But as it grows in importance, both economically and socially, rules emerge.'

– KOOS BEKKER, 2021[2]

IN 1952, JOSEPH STALIN STILL HAD AN IRON GRIP ON THE SOVIET Union, and Mao Zedong was becoming the undisputed despot of the People's Republic of China. That was the year Koos Bekker was born. Afrikaners of his generation grew up with the notion of the 'Rooi Gevaar' – the constant threat of communism.

Many South Africans believed that communism threatened not only private ownership, but also religious freedom. Congregations prayed for those trapped behind the Iron Curtain, and missionaries were funded to go on daring expeditions deep into Russia and China.

There was also a religious fervour in the way politicians sold the revolutionary regimes of communist states as hostile to democracy, even the apartheid version. The fact that Russians helped to train members of South Africa's liberation movements fed into the narrative, and married the concept of 'Swart Gevaar' – black majority rule – with 'Rooi Gevaar'.

A few decades later, after the ANC had won the first democratic election in 1994, Bekker would start pushing hard to invest in those very places that were demonised in his youth. The only thing was, the end of the Cold War did not necessarily mean the end of authoritarianism.

Vladimir Putin, a former member of the Soviet Union's notorious security agency the KGB, came to power in Russia in 2000. His first name means 'of great power', which foreshadowed his later ambitions. The world's largest country has held plenty of elections, but the outcome has never really been in doubt. Directly and indirectly, Putin has ruled for more than two decades.

China was still governed by the Communist Party, but to accelerate development, it started experimenting with free-market policies in parts of the country. The result was a technology boom and the establishment of giants such as Tencent, Alibaba and Baidu.

In the early 2000s, both Russia and China started signalling to the world that they were open for business. The message was and remains: invest in us, but play by our rules.

Bekker answered the call. In 2001, Naspers made that bet on Tencent. Five years later, Bekker and his team bought a 30 per cent stake in the Russian internet business Mail.ru.

'Mail is a nice company. When we got involved they were basically doing emails, and that gave them a massive audience but no real revenue,' said Bekker in 2010.[3]

But making money on emails was tough, as most people don't want to see advertisements while reading messages from friends. So Mail used its audience to start a portal.

'They became the biggest Russian-speaking portal ... In total there are about 300 million or so people that can understand Russian in some fashion, and then about 200 million that you could regard as the core market,' Bekker explained.[4]

The company branched out into online games and social networking. Before long it was the biggest games company in the Russian-speaking world. And its social networks were soon more popular than Facebook, Instagram or Twitter. VKontakte, which combines elements of Spotify's music catalogue and YouTube's video-sharing with a feed similar to that of Facebook, became the market leader among teenagers, while Odnoklassniki (the Russian word for 'classmates') mopped up the adults.

By November 2010, it was clear that Bekker had made a good investment. Mail.ru debuted on the LSE with a market cap of $5,4 billion, valuing Naspers's (by then) 29 per cent stake at $1,5 billion, almost three times the amount invested.

In March 2022, however, Naspers and Prosus wrote the investment down to zero. Putin had invaded Ukraine. Russian forces reduced cities in its neighbour to rubble, claiming thousands of civilian lives. The United States, the United Kingdom and the European Union responded with tough sanctions against Russia, targeting companies as well as individuals. Shares in Mail, which had been renamed VK Group in 2021, were suspended from trading on the LSE in early March.

The company's social media sites had been on the front lines of a battle for hearts and minds for years. Russian authorities impose stiff penalties on individuals who post content deemed 'illegal' – this usually means anything unkind to the Kremlin. The company that owns the site in question could be fined up to 10 per cent of annual revenue for not taking down such posts quickly enough.[5]

Shortly after the start of hostilities, VKontakte blocked imprisoned opposition leader Alexei Navalny's page for reportedly containing anti-war messages.[6] The Kremlin did not view its intervention in Ukraine as a war, preferring to describe it as a 'special military operation'. Censorship was nothing new, but Human Rights Watch reckoned it reached new heights as authorities blocked access to media sites based on their report-ing on the war. Major independent media outlets were also closed down.[7]

With television and radio mostly under state control, social media had been a useful tool for registering dissent and organising protests. In 2021, however, legislation was introduced that tightened the grip of censors and made VKontakte, Facebook and its peers responsible for enforcing these measures.

In 2022, both the Americans and Europeans slapped sanctions on VK CEO Vladimir Kiriyenko, son of Russia's former prime minister. Kiriyenko had run the company since entities linked to the state-owned energy giant Gazprom had taken control the previous year.[8] That's basically like Eskom acquiring Mxit. Why would the state want to be involved in social media?

Naspers and Prosus moved quickly to put daylight between themselves and their investment, resigning their board seats and making it clear that they had nothing to do with VK's day-to-day operations.

Just before trading in the VK Group was suspended, the company was worth only about as much as Naspers had piled into it over the years.

'In total we have invested about $700 million, but we've also received $500 million in dividends,' CFO Basil Sgourdos stated in March 2022.[9]

Down to zero just like that? Actually, the run-up was quite a bit longer. In 2013, Bekker trekked a few hours south of Moscow to visit Yasnaya Polyana, the birthplace and writing home of Leo Tolstoy. (Billionaire, yes, but an Afrikaans literature honours graduate first and foremost.) And when it comes to writing, there's no bigger superstar than this Russian. At the time of Bekker's visit, the first element in Tolstoy's monumental *War and Peace* was already brewing.

Ukrainians had for years been objecting to Russian influence over their politics, but when, in November 2013, President Viktor Yanukovych refused to sign a free-trade and political association agreement with the European Union, professing closer ties with Russia instead, protests erupted across the country. After violent clashes, Yanukovych was ousted in February the next year. Almost immediately, Russia invaded the Crimean Peninsula, a region in the south-east of Ukraine where nearly two-thirds of the inhabitants speak Russian instead of Ukrainian. Putin's government also recognised the self-declared republics of Donetsk and Luhansk, both of which were controlled by pro-Russia groups.

'Recently, uncertainty has risen due the volatile situation caused by events in Russia/Ukraine,' Naspers stated in its 2014 annual report.[10] The company was, of course, playing on both sides of the fence.

Though Ukraine has not featured much in Naspers's results or annual reports over the years, the company has built a useful business in this nation of 45 million people. It started in 2008 with the acquisition of the Poland-based e-commerce business Tradus. This company's Allegro division was exposed to several lucrative countries in the region. 'Its expanding markets are Czech (Republic), Hungary, Ukraine and Russia,' Bekker said at the time.[11]

In 2011, Naspers pushed in deeper, paying $29 million for Slando, a Ukrainian online classifieds site started by the founders of Gumtree.[12] The business was soon stitched into the OLX Group.

Slando also had a presence in Russia which gave Bekker and his team the opportunity to acquire a stake in Avito, a classifieds business seen by analysts as one of the best in Naspers's sprawling portfolio. Before the start of hostilities in 2022, Sgourdos valued Avito at some $6 billion. It was paying dividends and provided nearly a fifth of Prosus's free cash flow at the time. But sanctions meant that profits would be impossible to extract for an uncertain length of time.[13]

What to do? 'Prosus will have no day-to-day involvement in the operations of the business and will neither invest further nor seek to benefit economically from the interest in Avito in these circumstances,' the company stated. It decided to cease all involvement in its Russian operations and to decouple it from the rest of OLX.

'The separation process is under way which will decouple the companies into two independent entities. Avito will operate as an independent Russian entity run by a local management team, and governed by its own Board of Directors,' Prosus added.[14] Like cutting a spot out of a leopard? In May 2022, Prosus announced that Avito was for sale, signalling the end of the Russian adventure Bekker had embarked upon more than a decade earlier.[15]

Meanwhile, in Ukraine Prosus had 350 OLX employees and a business with grim prospects. '[O]ur Ukrainian operation will underperform until the political and economic situation there has stabilised, despite the long-term potential of this market and our solid position,' Naspers stated in its 2015 annual report.[16]

By 2022, it looked like those seven lean years would be followed by seven even leaner ones as millions of Ukrainian consumers fled to neighbouring countries. The devastation of bombed cities was also sure to weigh on the economy.

Bekker has on occasion praised the Russian education system and the quality of the nation's engineers. He has also remarked how Naspers did not carry the same baggage as American companies when venturing into new markets. However, he has not acknowledged quite so openly that, over the years, Naspers has been willing to do business in some rather authoritarian parts of the world.

As a platform for buying and selling, Avito is a relatively clean business. VK, with its ever-closer ties to Russia's ruling elite, is a different story.

'[S]ocial networks is Facebook's field, it's very hard to set up barriers to attack. So you can hide in Russia, like, behind culture and the Cyrillic script and so on, and it offers you a little bit of a defence,' Bekker explained in 2012.[17] Another useful barrier: authorities who are quite hostile to foreign firms. A decade later, Facebook was banned and VK's sites became just about the only gig in town.

After years of Naspers and Prosus pocketing dividends, and being not too bothered by the censorship, it took a war for the company to distance itself from VK. Bekker's 'dance with the devil' in Russia seemed to have cost billions, and left billions more on the table. In the end, sanctions by the world's financial policymakers were the reason the music stopped so suddenly.

In China, Naspers's biggest asset was nearly a hundred times the size of VK. But with Tencent it is not a case of foreign authorities pulling the plug on a slow song. Naspers's problem in China is that it has a dance partner with an uncomfortably firm grip.

From the start, investing in Chinese tech was no normal *sokkiejol* (dance party). When, in 2000, Hans Hawinkels spotted Tencent and alerted Bekker to its potential, a stake could only be held through a very specific structure.

Chinese government regulations prevent foreign firms from owning certain companies or assets. At the turn of the century, however, the listing of a few internet businesses required a structure that would allow Chinese companies access to foreign capital without officially selling shares to those investors. The result was the variable interest entity (VIE).

Simply put, this is a set of contracts that enables a foreign company to receive the economic benefits of operating a business in China. But there is no control, and in the end the investor does not own an actual share in the company.

Those were the rules in China at the turn of the century, and by 2022 they were still in place. An insightful joke doing the rounds on social media riffs off the tagline of Swiss watchmaker Patek Philippe: 'You never actually own a Chinese stock. You merely look after it for the Politburo.'[18]

The Chinese government's perceived tougher stance on big tech since 2020 has made many investors nervous. At the 2021 Naspers annual general meeting, some of them quizzed the Naspers board about VIEs and the way the company holds its stake in Tencent.

Bekker passed the question on to Charles Searle, the executive responsible for listed internet investments, who described the VIE as a pioneering structure that had played a crucial role in the development of the internet in China.[19] That's a diplomatic way of saying: so far, so good.

'Basically all major internationally listed Chinese companies follow these structures, and they have been stable for a very long period of time,' Searle declared.[20] Simply put: everyone else is doing it, so why shouldn't we?

'The importance of these structures and the crucial role that they play, continues to be very widely acknowledged in China,' he said, adding that recent remarks by the CSRC, China's financial services regulator, affirmed it. Basically: we have no other choice but to leave it to the government in Beijing – they call the shots.[21]

'VIE has been around for a very long period of time and we are not aware of any changes in the pipeline,' he continued.[22] Or: hold thumbs this thing lasts.

So Naspers, through Prosus, by mid-2022 held holds 29 per cent of Hong Kong-listed Tencent. But it didn't really 'own' 29 per cent of that stellar business on mainland China – the real Tencent.

Should this be seen as a major risk? Yes and no.

VIEs are the only way to wriggle into China. There is no other way to gain exposure to Chinese internet companies. The problem is more with the general unpredictability of the regulatory regime.

At the same meeting, Bekker shrugged off worries about China. 'In our sector, regulations are increasing everywhere,' he told shareholders.[23] He likened it to the first cars on the road that required no driving licences, no brake lights and no safety belts. 'That came only gradually as cars multiplied and got faster. The same happened with banking, with telecoms, pharmaceuticals, every major industry.'

In China, online games are so popular that the authorities make rules about the time children are allowed to spend playing them. And the onus is on the companies supplying the entertainment to monitor game time and restrict young players to a predetermined number of hours a day.

With gaming responsible for nearly a third of Tencent's revenue, its share price has often reacted sharply to announcements by the Chinese government, or even just editorials in state-owned media denouncing the youth's alleged addiction to mobile games.

'Fluctuations are expected in a fast-moving turbulent industry like ours still finding its feet. China is absolutely no exception,' Bekker added.[24]

He pointed at Facebook's 30 per cent dip eighteen months earlier due to regulatory threats and the early effects of the Covid-19 pandemic, and how it had since recovered to double the trough.

A bit of turbulence? When Bekker made his comment in August, shares in Tencent were already down 40 per cent from its high early in 2021. And the stock sank a further 30 per cent in the seven months that followed. To be fair, share prices are a moving target; it is the underlying business environment that really matters.

While the behaviour of big tech in the United States and Europe can hardly be described as angelic, oversight is at least more transparent. Remember Facebook founder Mark Zuckerberg awkwardly answering questions from members of the US Congress in 2018? Imagine the same thing in China.

Naspers CEO Bob van Dijk echoed Bekker's sentiment. 'There is a natural desire of every government to play a more meaningful role in the consumer internet,' he told the *Financial Mail* in 2021.[25] This doesn't sound scary at all.

However, fines by Chinese authorities for transgressions involving anything from music streaming to private education to fintech have weighed heavily on sentiment. Sometimes, vague announcements have the same effect. The reason: China has shown that no one is untouchable.

In 2020, regulators pulled the plug on Alibaba founder Jack Ma's plans to float Ant Group in Hong Kong and Shanghai. The initial public offering (IPO) was estimated to be worth some $37 billion, and would have made the listing the biggest yet.

Days before it was set to happen, Ma was summoned to a closed-door meeting in Beijing. This was not long after he had said at a conference that 'without risk, no innovation can happen in this world', a statement at odds with the thinking of China's government at the time.[26] The day after the meeting, Ant's IPO was cancelled, and the entity had to be restructured in line with the wishes of the central bank and financial regulators. It would be treated as a bank, not a fintech company.

Just like that, Chinese authorities took the sort of action that puts the fear of Mammon into investors.

Tencent's Pony Ma, on the other hand, has played it better. His company has been fined here and there, but has escaped severe sanctions. He has since 2013 been a delegate to the Communist Party's National People's Congress, and in 2021 even used this platform to call for the tighter regulation of internet businesses.[27]

In 2017, Tencent released a mobile game ahead of the party's conference not too subtly aimed at impressing the nation's leader. Titled 'Clap for Xi Jinping', the goal was to tap the screen as many times as possible in a limited time, simulating applause. It was, quite literally, a hit. And it showed that Tencent was on board with the government's plans, whatever they may be.

No wonder then that, early in 2020, Tencent complied with directives to censor hundreds of keywords on its WeChat super app related to the government's handling of Covid-19. The information handed over led to arrests and punishments. This was not new. In 2017, a man was given a prison sentence for calling Xi a 'steamed bun' in a private message to friends, the *Financial Times* reported.[28]

'We've always been treated very well by the Chinese government, and in many ways the country is more free than many others in the world,' Bekker said in 2010.[29]

For years he and Naspers were quite comfortable not to criticise censorship in either Russia or China, or say anything in public about the political situation in those countries.

'One might say, generously, that this is a pragmatic attitude learnt while surviving censorship in South Africa. Or, less generously, one might say that it reflects Naspers's history as a media company happy to live close to power,' wrote Bekker watcher Anton Harber in 2012.[30]

Investing in authoritarian regimes might be lucrative, but some extreme risks accompany it. Either the world can turn against the country you are investing in, or the country can turn against the company you have bought a stake in. Either way, it's a delicate dance to make those billions and to keep them.

14.

GO BIG WHEN YOU CAN AFFORD TO LOSE

'I lived in Holland for six years. If you go bankrupt in Holland, it's a scandal that engulfs the family; your mother will complain that you've destroyed the family reputation in the street. In America, if you go bankrupt, you smile; life goes on, next year you will have a success.'

– KOOS BEKKER, 2007[1]

'You know, now I am in my sixties. I can no longer risk everything I have, because I won't be able to start over.'

– KOOS BEKKER, 2021[2]

K OOS BEKKER JOKES THAT HE PLAYED CRICKET AT SCHOOL WITH 'considerable enthusiasm, but a distinct lack of talent'.[3] This was self-deprecatingly modest for the former captain of his school's first team. And judging by the way he approached his career, he was the sort of batsman who would play a few aggressive shots early in an innings.

For one, he decided on a career change at the age of twenty-five. After completing an LLB at Wits University, he started working in Soweto as a state prosecutor. He spent only two days in court before he decided that the human suffering and the stifling bureaucracy were not for him. After just three weeks, he was out.[4]

'I was tasked with prosecuting a woman who had poured boiling water over her husband. But he deserved it, so I let her go. A good prosecutor would have nailed her ...' he recalled later.[5]

Despite having studied law for half a decade, he decided to pad up for business instead. So he moved to Cape Town and started working in advertising. 'I did not want to learn a limited set of values – I wanted a school where I could learn from lots of people, and market research is one of the best places to learn,' he told an interviewer in 1990.[6]

His first project in advertising was to examine gherkin-eating habits. He found that women in Sea Point liked their gherkins sweeter and spicier than those in Newlands.[7]

'I respect advertising people for that subtlety of distinguishing consumer tastes, and I think it helped me later in business and in media also,' he said.

But marketing and advertising would also not become his career. The violence and instability in South Africa at that time convinced many young professionals to build a life elsewhere, so emigration rates soared.

As mentioned, Bekker sold his house, borrowed what he could and went to the United States for an MBA at Columbia University. His wife, Karen, bagged a job at a good magazine. They were not planning on coming back. His old friend Cobus Stofberg was also working in the Big Apple, plying his trade in finance at the broadcaster CBS.

After applying and lobbying for jobs in TV, Bekker finally landed the one he wanted at the pay-TV network HBO. Remember how he got to know all those executives while doing that final business school project on how to establish a pay-TV business outside the United States? Now he could follow the same career path.

'I imagined myself in my fifties, VP for Affiliate Relations at HBO, with a comb-over and a house in Connecticut ...' he told an interviewer two decades later.[8] Or he could try to hit the ball back over the bowler's head. And he thought, what the hell, why not try that pay-TV idea in South Africa?

That was when he pinged Ton Vosloo. After some serious pitching, he got the nod to start M-Net.

'[W]hen you're thirty, then you say, okay, what if we try this and it fails, then I start something else, because I don't have much to lose and I have my life ahead of me. The fact that we were so young meant we took enormous risks,' Bekker recalled.[9]

You are reading this book because Bekker did not lose. In fact, he won big. M-Net took less than half a decade to succeed spectacularly in an otherwise feeble economy. When pay-TV was enough of a success, Bekker started looking for the next big thing.

'We felt we had it in us to do more,' he said.[10] So he sent a team from the subscriber management division MultiChoice to look at the latest technological developments abroad, to see where the company should be investing.

Ian Wilkinson, who would later become M-Net CEO, went to the United States. He reported back that 'there is something you can put in the boot of your car and you could make cell-phone calls to your secretary'.[11]

Wilkinson and Karel Pienaar, who would end up spending more than two decades at MTN, championed the project and soon had Britain's Cable & Wireless (C&W) on board as an international partner. Then the lobbying began.

Telecommunications, like broadcasting, is a tightly regulated sector. Again, Bekker had Vosloo as a valuable ally to do the footwork with the authorities. However, the government told Vosloo and Bekker that it would only grant them an operating licence if they partnered with the state-controlled fixed-line provider, Telkom.

In October 1991, M-Net and C&W presented a proposal to Telkom, suggesting they join forces to develop a cellular service in South Africa. But the state-owned firm, which had a cushy monopoly over the nation's 4 million landline users, thought M-Net's projection of 300 000 clients was much too bullish. It estimated that only about 18 000 people, and no more, would see the use in a cellphone.[12]

The government of the day tapped auditing and consulting firm Coopers & Lybrand to suggest how the country's telecommunications services sector should be restructured to keep track with technological developments and a changing political climate. When the firm's report came out in 1992, it suggested, among other things, that two cellular licences be issued and that one should have Telkom as a major shareholder. M-Net again approached the fixed-line operator. And again it got no love.

Those were the years of the political transition. The ANC and its allies in the trade unions were dead set against the white minority government's plans to grant licences if it did not involve black participants. M-Net read the room and soon had the early black empowerment group NAIL on board as partner, alongside C&W and state-owned Transnet.

Despite the earlier setbacks, Vosloo remained undeterred and kept engaging with the authorities. 'After many peregrinations and compromises, two cellular network licences were finally awarded in 1994,' he recalls.[13]

A consortium that included Vodafone, the Rupert family's Rembrandt Group and Telkom got the nod to start Vodacom. The other licence went to the M-Net consortium – the result was MTN, which by 2021, had 32 million subscribers in South Africa alone.

In the 1990s, however, Bekker did not have the necessary capital to stay in MTN. M-Net and Naspers sold out of the cellular provider in 1999 to double down on pay-TV and the internet. He went big, and when he couldn't afford it anymore, he walked away.

Around the same time that he encouraged M-Net executives to dabble in cellular telephony, he took another big punt himself. Remember how Bekker says he was lucky to make money at thirty? Listing M-Net on the JSE and the windfall it brought him and his co-founders, Stofberg and Jac van der Merwe, gave him the opportunity to bat even more aggressively. So he took his family to the Netherlands.

Stofberg, Van der Merwe and Antonie Roux joined him in Amsterdam. From there they tried to build a pan-European pay-TV business. With FilmNet, Bekker was initially targeting six countries, but within half a decade the business had done several deals. As NetHold, in a new structure with Johann Rupert's Richemont, it was operating in more than a dozen markets on the continent. At that time, South Africa still had tight exchange controls, making it just about impossible to invest money offshore. But Richemont, based in Switzerland, earned its own cash abroad through the sale of cigarettes and luxury items such as Cartier watches and Montblanc pens. Rupert had also already invested in Telepiù, a pay-TV business in Italy.

NetHold was a corporate version of a bring-and-braai. Rupert brought the meat; Bekker and his team, backed by Naspers, knew how to pack and turn the grid; and together they built a fire. Instead of a steak, each party got a stake. Naspers held 40 per cent of NetHold, Richemont held 50 per cent, and media group Johnnic, which published the *Sunday Times*, the remaining 10 per cent.

But the European business was very different from the original M-Net. In Europe, Bekker and his team did not have one government to deal with, but a gaggle of them. And satisfying consumer tastes in so many different cultures and languages was certainly more complex than re-searching the pickle palates of Sharon and Maude in Cape Town.

Though it sounds impressive to operate in so many countries, the sprawl required substantial resources to build a profitable business. And year after year, MultiChoice (and later MIH) indicated that losses should be expected for most of the rest of the decade.

Each of the markets also had its own issues. In Scandinavia Bekker had a competitor, and in the Netherlands cable-TV was already entrenched. So by 1995, after more than three years in Europe, most of his original investment in FilmNet had not yet broken even, with MultiChoice Belgium a profitable exception. Telepiù in Italy was still making losses, while the operations in Greece and Central Europe had lots of cash-guzzling ahead of them.

In the meantime, investors had become used to M-Net's stellar profits. Many who had backed MultiChoice gritted their teeth as they watched how much money was being ploughed into a risky business thousands of kilometres away, with the operating loss increasing threefold in a year to top R130 million by 1995.

In a sideswipe at impatient investors, Bekker declared it was accepted in other countries that development losses could continue for a few more years, but in South Africa it bore some repeating.[14] He must have realised, however, that too many small loss-making countries did not make for a good business, and that the continued roll-out of digital satellite broadcasting would require much more capital than Naspers and Richemont were willing to provide.

Telepiù especially was hardly performing like an Italian stallion, more like a Milanese mule, and Rupert wanted less exposure to what was becoming a big drag on the Richemont group's performance. 'Rob Hersov, CEO of Telepiù pay-TV at that time, advised Richemont to sell its stake,' Rupert disclosed in 2013.[15]

Bekker was still pushing to make the pan-European business viable, and wanted to pull in an investor with an even bigger warchest than his South African partner. He had been impressed by the launch of digital satellite dishes in the United States, where a company named DirecTV was taking the fight to cable broadcasters. DirecTV's success was part of Bekker's motivation to move so quickly from analogue to digital in South Africa.

By the mid-1990s, the Americans were snooping around Europe looking to extend their pay-TV empire to a new continent. They had deep pockets, stretching all the way back to General Motors (GM), then still one of the largest companies in the world. GM owned technology giant Hughes Electronics, which owned DirecTV in turn.

Soon a deal was on the table that would see DirecTV inject $1 billion into NetHold in exchange for a third of the business. A cool billion would go a long way towards realising NetHold's ambition to be Europe's pay-TV leader.

It would also be a serious blow to rivals with grand ambitions. At the time, Canal+ had a strong foothold in France, while Western Europe's two largest markets, Germany and the United Kingdom, were serviced by the joint venture between the Kirch Group and media mogul Rupert Murdoch's British Sky Broadcasting.

Though Bekker had $1 billion on the table from the Americans, Rupert apparently did not like the fine print of the proposed deal. And a meeting with John Malone, then CEO of Hughes, was not a pleasant one as the South African tobacco tycoon and the American 'Cable Cowboy' got into a verbal brawl.[16]

'Richemont therefore took the initiative,' says Rupert.[17] This meant it pounced when Canal+ started getting nervous about Americans lurking in its backyard.

Bekker was not the only one going big. France's Canal+ formed part of a business empire in the making. Flamboyant CEO Jean-Marie Messier, whom Bekker calls 'a little Napoleon', was stitching together a global giant.[18] The result would eventually be called Vivendi, a media and tele-communications Frankenstein that until the mid-1970s focused on supplying water to large cities. (Ironically, it would be a lack of liquidity that would end Messier's stint at the company in 2002.)

Could there be two better parties interested in your business? On the one side, there was GM-backed Hughes with bakkie-loads of cash. On the other was an ambitious CEO who would later be the focus of a book titled *The Man Who Tried to Buy the World*.[19]

'[S]ubsequent to a bidding war between Hughes DirecTV and Canal+, both Richemont and Naspers sold their holdings in Telepiu to Canal+,' Rupert records.

The deal went through phases with the South Africans initially holding a smaller stake of the larger business. But a later disagreement led to Messier buying NetHold's assets in Western and Central Europe for $2,2 billion (around R7 billion at the time). And they got out just in time. 'We were fortunate to get about €68 per share. A year later Vivendi was trading at less than €8 per share,' says Rupert.

Many have speculated that the Canal+ deal, seemingly lined up without Bekker's knowledge, caused a rift between the two soon-to-be billionaires. Both deny that such a 'divorce' took place, with Rupert describing

Bekker as a 'friend for decades', and Bekker saying that they had worked together very well for five years.

Bekker, a quarter of a century later, styles it as a 'collective decision' to cash in. 'In that way, we realised a huge profit, and for the first time got our own dollars to invest in the internet,' he later told *Fortunes* author Ebbe Dommisse. But the passage that precedes this one is quite interesting: 'Rupert maintained afterwards that he had spared Naspers huge embarrassment by selling NetHold to the French. It was even whispered from the Rupert camp that Naspers had been saved from bankruptcy.'[20]

Dommisse was, after all, the authorised biographer of Rupert's father, Anton, so he was more plugged in than most about how the deal was perceived on that side of the partnership. The younger Rupert later wrote that Telepiù finally racked up cumulative cash-flow losses in excess of €5.4 billion, and that the Richemont and Naspers share of that toxic mountain could have been in excess of €2.5 billion. That's the sort of loss that could torpedo many a newspaper publisher.

In the end, Bekker's five-year innings in Europe worked out well. He went big and earned his company its own pile of cash outside South Africa. And he bagged the top job at Naspers.

As CEO of the company that initially backed him, he could afford to go even bigger, opting to work for no salary and getting paid only in stock options (more in chapter 1). Though this meant he would make money only if the company performed, it also exposed him to the greatest possible personal upside.

He used Naspers's newly acquired foreign cash pile to make some gutsy investments in the Far East – and lost nearly all of it. Fortunately for him, and for South African investors and pensioners, Tencent stuck, and Naspers has mostly held on to it ever since.

As Naspers grew under Bekker, first thanks to the contribution of M-Net and MultiChoice, and later due to Tencent's impressive run, the company gained the means to pile more into each deal. As a behemoth, it could now afford to lose amounts that would have sunk it only a decade earlier.

A loss from a failed investment that might seem huge in rand or dollar terms was not so big in relative terms.

What's more, Bekker eventually acquired the personal capital he needed to build a whole new portfolio of businesses. This personal capital was a combination of his reputation for creating wealth and his firm grip on decision-making at the company he headed.

The practice of ploughing billions from MultiChoice and Tencent into e-commerce assets started when he was CEO, but has continued under his chairmanship. By 2022, more than $7 billion had been invested in food delivery, some $6,7 billion in online payments and fintech, $6,5 billion in electronic classifieds, and more than $3 billion in education technology (edtech).[21]

Many investors still see the e-commerce portfolio as spectacular value destruction: taking dividends from Tencent – or even worse, selling down the stake in China's greatest company – to acquire and fund businesses that will take years to generate decent returns, if at all.

Ironically, Naspers, through Prosus, sold a 2 per cent sliver of Tencent for nearly HKD600 per share in April 2021. But in the months thereafter, Tencent stock declined substantially, due to what investors see as a crackdown by China on its large tech companies. By mid-March 2022, Tencent had dipped to below HKD300 per share.

An optimist may see the push by Bekker and his successor as Naspers CEO into food delivery, classifieds, payments and edtech as a way of diversifying away from Tencent. Bekker himself predicted that, by 2020, Naspers's unlisted e-commerce portfolio could be much bigger than its listed investments, which included Tencent.

Perhaps Bekker is simply approaching the business in a similar way to his personal fortune. For many years, almost all his wealth was in Naspers stock. During his two sabbaticals he disposed of millions of shares, and diversified his holdings to some extent. But what to do with the proceeds? Would he have found a better home for his cash in South Africa than Naspers shares?

Compared to Naspers, anything he did with his personal fortune could probably be seen, quite harshly, as wealth destruction. Like ploughing cash into agriculture. 'Koos reads widely and is a keen traveller, and he wastes money on farming,' reads a short bio, presumably written by himself, in 2007.[22] But by the time Bekker went big on plums and wine at Babylonstoren, his historic estate in the Cape Winelands, he could afford to lose a million or two.

15.

EVOLVE THE BUSINESS PHILOSOPHY

'Whatever the cause may be of each slight difference in the offspring from their parents – and a cause for each must exist – it is the steady accumulation, through natural selection, of such differences, when beneficial to the individual, that gives rise to all the more important modifications of structure, by which the innumerable beings on the face of this earth are enabled to struggle with each other, and the best adapted to survive.'

– CHARLES DARWIN, 1859[1]

'People quote Darwin saying that it is the strongest that survive, the fittest. But that is not what he said: he said it is those who are most flexible, those who can adapt to change, who survive.' – KOOS BEKKER, 2012[2]

IN THE PREFACE TO THIS BOOK, BEKKER IS QUOTED AS REFERRING to recipes for success as 'dangerous'. He also told the interviewer: 'In reality, a human baby comes into this world with almost nothing in its head – one advantage your brain has to that of an ant is precisely that it is reprogrammable. You learn from events.'[3] During a career spanning four decades, he had many events to learn from.

As a student and young professional, Bekker experienced the oil price shocks and rampant inflation of the 1970s as well as the boom and bust of the gold price rally that accompanied it. He lived through the instability and violence of the later stages of South Africa's political conflict, and the international isolation that followed. He saw the advent of television in South Africa, the fall of communism in Europe, and the rise of corporate governance principles. More importantly, he lived through the start of the internet, the end of apartheid, and the re-emergence of China as a major political and economic powerhouse.

Most of these changes brought business opportunities with them. An increasingly ossified, controlled and moralising state monopoly on TV prepared the soil for an entertaining alternative such as M-Net. When the Iron Curtain was drawn open in the early 1990s, the light fell on new markets in Europe. Sleeping giant China woke up more hungry than grumpy. And the internet surprised the world in the late 1990s with its slow pace in developing real business applications, and again with its rapid acceleration in the 2010s.

From early on, Bekker saw M-Net as the beginnings of something bigger. 'We want to use pay-TV to create a foothold; the next step will be to start a radio station, then to get into electronic databases,' he declared in 1986.[4]

Though M-Net's radio plans never went live, Bekker did have a go at stitching data into the business. Only months after listing on the JSE, M-Net acquired Information Trust Corporation (ITC). It was one of those strange opportunities that sprouted from the disinvestment campaigns in apartheid's final decade. ITC was actually the remnants of the South African branch of Dun & Bradstreet, an American data business.

But for Bekker the future lay not in going deeper into South Africa, grabbing a larger slice of an isolated pie. The real opportunities lay in using locally tested knowledge and expertise and applying it in other markets. An entire world was opening up.

He was right about using pay-TV as a foothold. With a partner, he tried building a global business from Europe, but could not get to scale quickly enough. When they cashed out, Bekker had money for acquisitions, but almost no other viable pay-TV investment options. So he used the existing business in Africa, the Middle East and the Mediterranean to keep generating cash while investing in the Far East and specifically China, which was opening up to foreign capital.

As noted earlier, he then made the error of sending in Western managers. This lost Naspers some serious money. A related mistake was thinking that Naspers needed to be an operator wherever it went.

M-Net was a success because Bekker and his team built it from the ground up. They designed a company in South Africa for the South African market, to be run by South Africans. In effect, Naspers backed local management: Bekker, Cobus Stofberg and Jac van der Merwe. The press groups that pushed in millions in the 1980s just happened to be local too.

It would take Bekker some time to identify that philosophy. As Naspers CEO, he learnt from China to back local people who knew their markets and 'how to deal with things there'.[5]

This also meant being willing to be a foreign investor without actually having control. Naspers missed out on several unicorns in the early 2000s because Bekker was unwilling to take a minority stake (see chapter 10). Who knows, a decade or so later Naspers might have backed a young Alibaba, NetEase or LinkedIn.

Functioning like a true angel investor, piling in money when someone has a mere idea, carries a failure rate of about 80 per cent, Bekker said in 2014. 'That's too high for us. But if you wait until a company is successful, it's too late, there is no money to be made,' he added.[6]

Part of Naspers's evolution was learning what the company did well. Starting from scratch in foreign markets was not the way to go, but neither was acquiring mature businesses. Bekker took his time feeling out how to be an investor in places such as Asia, Latin America and Russia. Eventually he settled on a model somewhere between venture capital and America's big-tech approach.

'A venture capital (VC) fund will walk in and say, give me 5 per cent. They don't hassle you very much, except they look for every opportunity to cash out. They want to force you into an IPO and so on, and they don't contribute that much. When they run, they run,' he explained in 2009.[7]

This can leave entrepreneurs stranded, and hamper the development of a business to its full potential. It was Tencent's frustration with venture capital funders that opened the door for a new investor in 2000 and changed Bekker's destiny. So he wanted to be better than a VC.

Some of the other investors that compete with Naspers, especially the American tech giants, employ a different approach. 'So Google would typically buy out 100 per cent of a company and integrate it into the bigger Google, which is valid for them,' he told eNCA interviewer Chris Gibbons in 2014.[8]

But media have a social, cultural and even political component, and big technology is facing increased scrutiny from local regulators because of the volumes of sensitive data handled by the likes of Facebook, Google and others. This means that there are parts of the world where Silicon Valley's champions are either not welcome or not comfortable.

Also, according to Bekker, it counts against American companies that they wade in with fleets of limousines and act as big shots in towns that are not used to that sort of behaviour.[9] It has served his company well to be low-key.

Under Bekker, Naspers found its sweet spot where there are five to twenty employees, some revenue, but no great profit. Companies with solid management that need money. 'And we take let's say 30 per cent or so of the business. We like backing entrepreneurs who stay in the business.'[10]

In describing the people and ventures his company wants to invest in, Bekker may just as well be reading his own CV. 'Naspers wants someone in charge with a vested interest, not a bureaucrat. Bureaucrats' aspirations are a bigger office, a more expensive car – while someone with skin in the game will look after the company's profits,' he said in 2009.[11]

Bekker would then move in and get Naspers seats on the board and the audit committee. The investor helped the business operationally where it could, but with a long-term mindset. 'This works for entrepreneurs who need cash and linkage to a larger pool of experience, but who don't want to lose control of their babies,' Bekker explained.[12]

And when he found the right person, team and company, he was willing to hold on for decades. 'We tend to back a number of entrepreneurs that we believe in and then stay with them for the next 20 years. So our failure rate will be 40 per cent or 50 per cent, but the winner is there to make up for the losers.'[13] Tencent, of course, is the poster child for the winner.

Since the early 2000s, Naspers has been content with 100 per cent local management and often local partners, Bekker told an interviewer in 2008. Local means people who hail from the country Naspers is investing in. 'The Americans aren't happy with that. They like to run the show, and we are more used to operating as a partner in a multiple entity.'[14]

For many years, a big part of Bekker's strategy was using South Africans to go and seek out those opportunities. Remember how he and his team went to Amsterdam to have a go at building a European pay-TV empire, and how Hans Hawinkels and Charles Searle explored media and internet opportunities in the Far East? Naspers business led to Antonie Roux living in Italy, the Netherlands and Thailand. And the business sent Basil Sgourdos to the Far East. All of them cut their teeth at M-Net or MultiChoice during those companies' exciting first decade.

The company attracted cowboys, people who were prone to taking risk, as mentioned in an earlier chapter.

But shooting from the hip also leads to a few misses. Fortunately, Tencent's success has overshadowed some of the failures. And being close to the Chinese giant has helped Naspers push into industries it might otherwise have overlooked.

Many investors, however, wish Naspers had never embarked on Bekker's mission of building an e-commerce portfolio alongside Tencent. In 2021, the company first published a value for this multidenominational church of businesses – some $39 billion.

But this was after the Covid-19-fuelled tech boom that accompanied the throttling lockdowns and unprecedented economic stimulus measures in much of the world. Whether the opinions of sell-side analysts are a good measure of value for unlisted assets in food delivery, electronic classifieds, online payments and education technology spread over 120 countries remained to be seen.

However, Prosus's acquisitive spree since the start of the pandemic has indicated a willingness to depart from Bekker's earlier plans to mostly dip into emerging markets and to take substantial, though non-controlling, stakes in fledgling businesses.

Most computer programmers and app developers in South Africa know Stack Overflow, and many will have a tab open in a forum to help them work through coding problems. But few are aware that it is controlled from Cape Town. Prosus paid $1.8 billion for 100 per cent of the business in June 2021.

What's more, Stack Overflow is a New York-based company, so the notion of treading into pioneer markets hardly seems valid.

'We've admired the company for a long time,' says Prosus's head of edtech, Larry Illg.[15] But if Prosus had known about it for so long, why only invest when it did?

At twenty-two times revenue – not even profit – $1.8 billion is a steep valuation for Stack Overflow, says Flagship Asset Management's Pieter Hundersmarck.[16]

Prosus also paid $1 billion more for the business than the amount it was valued at less than a year earlier. What's more, CEO Bob van Dijk, Illg and their team bought Stack Overflow from Andreessen Horowitz, Spark Capital and Silver Lake, some of Silicon Valley's most savvy investors. Why would they sell if it was such an attractive asset?

'The deal just looks like value destruction,' says Hundersmarck.[17] Far from picking a filly with a bump on its forehead and helping it grow,

Naspers and Prosus suddenly seemed to be shovelling cash at takeover targets and creating instant unicorns.

Not only Stack Overflow but also the other edtech investments seem to signal a change in strategy for Prosus. In the past, and with its other e-commerce segments, the group had mostly started with modest investments, says Old Mutual Investments portfolio manager Neelash Hansjee. 'Now they are spending big amounts of money – large cheques – upfront, for controlling shareholdings.'[18]

A few months later, Prosus selected India's payments business BillDesk and clicked 'add to cart' for \$4,7 billion. Again, it bought 100 per cent of the company and made founders MN Srinivasu, Ajay Kaushal and Karthik Ganapathy very rich. And it was the biggest acquisition thus far for either Prosus or Naspers.

The deal was billed as extending the reach into online payments and going deeper into the lucrative financial services market. Prosus cited expectations that 200 million new consumers would latch on to digital payments in India over the following three years, and per capita volumes would rise tenfold to 220 transactions a year.

These are lofty projections. And they probably need to be realised to justify forking out as much as the value of, say, South Africa's Discovery for an Indian fintech company.

With annual turnover of \$200 million, and a modest profit of \$37 million, BillDesk's revenue and earnings multiples seem steep at twenty-four and 125 times respectively. These are the sorts of numbers that make investment analysts gasp.

Even without a financial background, an onlooker could be forgiven for asking whether the nearly \$15 billion Prosus bagged from the sale of 2 per cent of Tencent only a few months earlier wasn't perhaps burning a hole in its pocket.

Most of top management at Naspers and Prosus now come from a management consulting background. Sure, the new faces have spent time at e-commerce businesses such as PayPal and eBay, and have high-class MBAs, but none of them has built a successful business from scratch.

In 2014, Bekker expanded on his comment about attracting cowboys: 'As you grow more established though a certain structure invades the company. You also start drawing different people ... As you grow, you get people who want to play it safe, who go for an established company with an established job. Your task as CEO then is to fight that, to try and keep a certain informality, a pioneer spirit, even though you're growing.'[19]

But he is now Naspers chair, and has to watch from a safe following distance how his business philosophy is being implemented.

Much larger than before, the group now also has a less South African flavour at the top. Van Dijk, Bekker's successor as Naspers CEO, is Dutch. And the heads of Prosus's four main business segments are all from the United States and France. CFO Basil Sgourdos and Charles Searle, who oversees the listed internet investments (basically Tencent and Russia's Mail), are the only South Africans with meaningful management roles outside of the domestic operations. That, perhaps, is the cost of evolving into a global giant.

Starting with a phone call to a newspaper boss, Bekker has built a business, transformed another and in the process created immense wealth for South Africans – be they pensioners, investors, his own colleagues or himself.

Successful people often reverse-engineer a strategy onto a fortunate set of events to explain their 'genius'. But Bekker knows better. 'I think in general business managers, when bad luck hits them, complain about fortune, and when they have a stroke of luck they usually attribute it to their own foresight,' he commented in 2009.[20]

When he retired as Naspers CEO five years later, Bekker gave this overview of his success at Naspers to *Rapport*'s Hanlie Retief: 'Our group could make short jumps from print media to pay-TV to cellular phones to the internet to e-commerce. With long jumps, you lose your balance. So, we look for something that will grow nicely but where, after a short jump, we can land on our feet.'[21]

It was not his only interview after hanging up his gloves as Naspers chief. In another, he commented on the highlights of his career, and said something that should be chiselled on the statue or tombstone of every billionaire: 'I think there is always an element of luck and circumstance.'[22]

AFTERWORD

I BOUGHT THREE SHARES. THIS WAS IN 2019, AND I WAS A HACK at the *Sunday Times*. Naspers had just announced it was lumping its consumer internet businesses together and listing it on the Euronext bourse in Amsterdam. If Koos Bekker was going to bang a gong at the world's oldest stock exchange, I wanted to be there.

Surely the company could not deny a shareholder access to the proceedings? Imagine the colour I could add to a Bekker book if I were present when the Naspers chair led the company into its next chapter. Forwards – the very meaning of the word 'Prosus'. It would soon be Europe's largest technology company. Among other things, management was billing the event as the beginning of Naspers's final reckoning with the dreaded 'discount'.

I had been to a few dozen stock market debuts on the JSE, and seen my fair share of board chairs and CEOs awkwardly blowing the kudu horn to get trading going. And I regretted not being there when Steinhoff International listed in Frankfurt half a decade earlier. While writing *Christo Wiese: Risk & Riches,* I thought, hell, what if the Steinhoff chair had said something memorable to CFO Ben la Grange on that day, but in Afrikaans. No one would have picked it up. If a tree falls in the forest … or more like, if an *Oom* says something in his own *taal,* but there is no one around to hear it, does it make a quote?

For me, the Prosus listing meant flying to Europe on my own dime. And probably on my own time too. After some haggling, I hammered out a deal with my employer to file all my regular stories and a Big Read feature about the listing and not have all three of those precious leave days deducted from my tally. Looking back on it now, I cut myself a pretty shitty deal. Not getting paid to work, but *paying* to work. To be honest, no South African media institution was going to send a reporter to Amsterdam to cover such a soft event. No matter how big the float, a bourse debut is a PR event.

So, if I was going to get there on my own steam, I had to at least make sure I could get in. That's why I bought those three Naspers shares. When the new company listed, I got three Prosus shares to boot.

Obviously the investment was declared to my employer's human resources department. In the dematerialised world of high-frequency trading, newspapers in South Africa somehow still believe they can move markets, and that a forty-year-old daft enough to work as a print journalist could make an illicit fortune from the rise or fall of three shares.

I won't tell you whether the whole exercise cost me more than a month's salary, or less. But I can share that I received a better return on the stock than on the visit to the stock exchange. (And that's saying a lot, because as I write this, my Naspers investment is under water and Prosus shares are also trading far below its listing price.)

I wanted to use the opportunity to strike up a conversation with Bekker. What better place to pitch an authorised biography? 'Koos, I'm your man. We'll do something similar to Phil Knight's *Shoe Dog*. Let's go deep into those first few years of M-Net. Give me access to your archives.' Best-seller for sure. And I would get to sit down with one of the nation's business greats. Maybe even take him on in chess (not sure what the outcome would be), or a game of Afrikaans Scrabble (certain to give the billionaire a proper drubbing).

But no Bekker on Beursplein that rainy September day in Amsterdam. Local boy Bob van Dijk was the one banging the gong. I hoped the supposedly media-shy media mogul might be lurking behind the scenes – but Naspers and Prosus staff assured me he was not there.

Little did I know it would be the last opportunity to see him before writing this book. Pandemics happen, apparently. And so my plans of buying Tencent stock and travelling to China for an AGM were scuppered by that combo of politics, 'science' and geography that has come to define the response to Covid-19 worldwide. Naspers's two most recent AGMs were also virtual events, with Bekker dialing in from London.

But that's not to say that I've never interacted with the man who built M-Net and transformed Naspers. Our paths have crossed at least seven times during the past two decades. There was a dinner, a lunch, a walk-by, a call, another call, an email and a third call.

The dinner was towards the end of 2002. Bekker had just started his second five-year contract as Naspers CEO, and the company had begun to recover from the devastation of the dotcom crash. I was all of twenty-two years old, and studying at Stellenbosch University. Not the most diligent of law students, and always looking for an excuse to speak in front of a crowd, I ran as a candidate in the Students' Representative Council (SRC) election. (Follow me for more recipes on how to torpedo an academic career.) A council representing students obviously does some important and satisfying work, but after four years of *koshuiskos* (res food), the meals with university dignitaries and sponsors were the real highlight. So much red wine. So much steak with a sauce of your choice. Quite literally training in gravy.

The worst winer-and-diner of the entire year? Naspers. Bekker hosting the SRC in Cape Town. Cocktails on the Nasdak. Stunning views of Cape Town. We sit down for supper. Each person in attendance (and their dates too!) is asked to give their view on the world – I wish I could recall the comments made by the boss. I do remember, however, that Bekker then announced something to the effect of: How lucky the Naspers board, management and editors are to dine with students, as it gives them all the excuse to eat junk food for a change.

Dinner was served: burgers and chips. Remember, this was years before the gourmet burger craze. Pretty ordinary stuff.

Lunch was two years later. I'd finally decided that law was not for me, and a career in journalism would be a better fit. Deadlines? No worries. Pay? Will figure that out later. In Stellenbosch, we were a class of about twenty postgrad journalism students. Naspers was an important source of funding for the department and used it to source new recruits for its magazines and newspapers. Not too deep into the year, we were told to schedule an hour in our calendars for lunch with the CEO. Again, putting my previous experience of a Naspers-sponsored meal down to bad luck, I was looking forward to something substantial.

Not to be. Bekker arrived, and we took a stroll. In an alley not far from the dive bars Tollies and Stones, we were escorted into a Chinese restaurant. Peking duck? Nope. Don't think Michelin-star Chinese, think Lucky Star Chinese. I reckon the whole thing set Naspers back less than the price of one share. Again, a speech. And I do recall Bekker saying something like: 'China is the future.'

Everyone probably has a memory or two linked specifically to a game during the 2010 FIFA World Cup. I can't recall which game it was, but it was in the Cape Town Stadium. I watched a few of them. Probably not Portugal's demolition of North Korea – more likely the knockout game between Germany and Argentina. Just like that, Bekker walks past. Bigwig, member of the local organising committee, on his own, South African scarf around the neck, giving me a nod of acknowledgement as he passes. Well, it could have been a nod.

By 2013, I was working for *The Times*, a spunky daily that had roped me in to write business stories for the mass market – whatever that means. When Naspers reported results, I set up a call with Bekker and CFO Steve Pacak. I could not shake the feeling that they must have thought they were granting an interview to *The Times* of London. I greeted Bekker in Afrikaans and then suggested we switch to English for the benefit of Pacak. Not necessary. Bekker said something like: He's been working here long enough to understand.

In 2019, I scavenged Bekker's cell number from a colleague. I needed colour for a piece about Naspers's decision to list (yet-to-be-named) Prosus in Amsterdam. I had written an intro, but I wanted to know whether the name of the Nasdak, the company's cocktail venue in Cape Town, was intended to be a wordplay on the American technology bourse, the Nasdaq. 'Obviously,' said Bekker, after first cautioning that any questions about the company should be directed at Van Dijk and management. So this is the intro I came up with:

> The 26th floor of the head office of Africa's biggest company is known as the "Nasdak" – a clever combination of "Naspers" and the Afrikaans word for roof, pronounced almost exactly like Nasdaq, the stock exchange in New York known for its tech stocks.
>
> At Naspers, this floor is a function venue boasting spectacular views of Table Mountain and Cape Town's harbour. A place where executives might be able to gaze out at the natural attractions and into the future beyond.
>
> The name was suggested by one of the hundreds of journalists who worked for SA's largest newspaper publisher in the early 2000s. Whether it was pure coincidence or revealed a deeper ambition, it foreshadowed Naspers's transformation from a print and pay-TV business into a consumer-facing technology giant. The kind of company that could be a big player on the Nasdaq.
>
> But this week, when the company shared its plans to hive off a part of its assets, it named not the Nasdaq but Amsterdam's Euronext exchange as its bourse of choice ...[1]

My phone rings a few weeks later. In a textbook example of *'Koos sê so'*, the man at the other end tells me that Bekker told him to find out who had thought up the name 'Nasdak'. After some digging, he could now reveal that it had been so-and-so, doing that job at this outpost of the Naspers empire. I never jotted down the details of what he said. I did, however, think it strange that the chair of a multinational enterprise worth so many billions would instruct someone to dig up such a peculiar nugget of information for a story in a rival newspaper.

Later that year, I decided to pitch a Bekker biography to my publishers. They were keen, but given that the subject was (and still is) the chair of their parent company, they just wanted to make sure it was all okay. I wrote up the idea in a document, and sent it off. The reply: sorry, no book about Koos.

So, I tested the waters at Penguin Random House. Write away. When? Right away.

Early in 2020, I pop Bekker an email, telling him that I am certainly going to write about him. No reply. I let it lie for a few months. Pandemics happen.

Then I give him a call. Bekker hears me out and says, *ja*, he's known plenty of people who have become famous, one way or the other. Didn't do them much good.

Sure, I say, but you're already famous. He disagrees. When queueing for a loaf of bread, he's still anonymous. I want to make a joke about *loafing* in retirement, but think better of it.

Bekker wasn't exactly friendly. Nor was he nasty. Just direct. He didn't say 'Bye'. Only: *'Beste.'*

ACKNOWLEDGEMENTS

THANK YOU TO MY DARLING WIFE LEJANIE WHO HAS KINDLY listened to my ramblings about this book pre-pandemic and post, pre-braai and post, pre-publication and will probably also post. Your love and support means everything.

A big shoutout to my commissioning editor, Marida Fitzpatrick, who elegantly bullied me into finishing the manuscript and had seen the statue of Koos in the boulder of info long before I did.

Louis Gaigher, your enthusiasm and insights about the finished chapters came at just the right time and thank you for your patience in getting KB's B over the line.

Thank you to rest of the team at Penguin Random House and especially Riaan de Villiers who did a stellar job in ironing out the creases in the manuscript.

And of course, thank you to everyone – analysts, journalists, tycoons, fans and critics – willing to speak to me about Koos and his creations.

If you bought this book, cheers.

NOTES

PREFACE

1   Hoër Volkskool Heidelberg, 'Ons Hoofseun aan die woord', Jaarblad, 1970. Original: 'En wat elkeen van ons mag bereik, sal nie slegs 'n bloot persoonlike prestasie wees nie, maar 'n prestasie waarin die Heidelbergse Volkskool ook sy aandeel gehad het.'

2   Koos Bekker, Address at Maastricht School of Management, Graduation Day, 9 September 2014, at https://www.youtube.com/watch?v=FP3eDRqcY24

3   *Forbes*, n.d, 'Profile: Koos Bekker', at https://www.forbes.com/profile/koos-bekker/?sh=2d993757416d

4   Shaun Harris, 'Going full circle', *Finance Week*, 12 June 1997.

5   kykNET, *Hannes aan Huis*, Onderhoud met Koos Bekker, Kwêla, 14 April 2021, at https://kyknet.dstv.com/program/kwela_275/kwela-koos-bekker/video

6   Ebbe Dommisse, *Fortunes: The rise and rise of Afrikaner tycoons*, Cape Town: Jonathan Ball, 2021, p. 71.

CHAPTER 1

1   Koos Bekker, 'Don't try this at home', Fin24, 11 May 2015, at https://www.news24.com/fin24/koos-bekker-dont-try-this-at-home-20150511

2   Koos Bekker, 'Sakegesprek met Theo Vorster', 16 October 2012, at https://www.youtube.com/watch?v=j o9brNP2tOo&list=PLF9AXykvyZ5Pf27 unIr_m-Gz3x3zFP66P&index=6

3   Ton Vosloo, *Across Boundaries: A life in the media in a time of change*, Cape Town: Jonathan Ball, 2018, pp. 34–35.

4   Shaun Harris, 'Going full circle', *Finance Week*, 12 June 1997.

5   Bekker, 'Sakegesprek met Theo Vorster'.

6   Michael C Jensen and William H Meckling, 'Theory of the firm: Managerial behavior, agency costs and ownership structure', *Journal of Financial Economics* 4 (4), October 1976, pp. 305–360.

7   Michael Jensen and Kevin Murphy, 'CEO incentives: It's not how much you pay, but how', *Harvard Business Review* 68 (3), 1999, pp. 138–149.

8   This was the Equity Expansion Act of 1993. Jay Matthews, 'Congress enters the fray over executive stock options rule', *Washington Post*, 13 August 1993.

9   Bekker, 'Don't try this at home'.

10 Bekker, 'Sakegesprek met Theo Vorster'.

11 Bekker, 'Don't try this at home'.

12 Naspers, Annual Report, 1996, p. 32.

13 Harris, 'Going full circle'.

14 Bekker, 'Don't try this at home'.

15 Moneyweb, 'Koos Bekker: From farmer's son to global digital success', 25 February 2016, at

https://www.moneyweb.co.za/moneyweb-radio/from-farmers-son-to-global-digital-success/

16 The company was called MIH Ltd and was part of a spider's web of businesses with similar-sounding names Naspers used for its dealings abroad.

17 Anton Harber, *Gorilla in the Room: Koos Bekker and the rise and rise of Naspers*, Johannesburg: Parktown Publishers, 2012, p. 19.

18 Tim Arringo, 'How the AOL-TimeWarner merger went so wrong', *The New York Times*, 10 January 2010.

19 Tammy Lloyd, 'New world explorer', *Financial Mail*, 6 October 2000, pp. 50–52.

20 Bekker, 'Don't try this at home'.

21 Koos Bekker, Address at Maastricht School of Management Graduation Day, 9 September 2014, at https://www.youtube.com/watch?v=FP3eDRqcY24

22 Bekker, 'Don't try this at home'.

23 Ibid.

24 Jeff Bezos, Statement to the US House Committee on the Judiciary, at https://blog.aboutamazon.com/policy/statement-by-jeff-bezos-to-the-u-s-house-committee-on-the-judiciary

25 Ibid.

26 Chris Buchanan, 'Koos Bekker: CEO Naspers – extract from today's interview on CNBC Africa's Power Lunch in association with Moneyweb', 11 April 2008, at https://www.moneyweb.co.za/archive/koos-bekker-ceo-naspers-9/

27 Ibid.

28 Ibid.

29 Ibid.

30 Naspers, Annual Report, 2008.

31 *Business Day TV*, 'Naspers: Koos Bekker', 26 February 2014.

32 Ann Crotty, 'Bekker's exquisite timing', *Business Times*, 11 October 2015.

33 Ryk van Niekerk, 'Options were specific to CEO role – Koos Bekker', Moneyweb, 21 September 2015, at https://www.moneyweb.co.za/news/companies-and-deals/options-were-specific-to-ceo-role-bekker/

34 Ibid.

35 Bekker, 'Don't try this at home'.

CHAPTER 2

1 Ton Vosloo, *Across Boundaries: A life in the media in a time of change*, Johannesburg: Jonathan Ball, 2018, p. 35.

2 Chris Barron, 'Everything he does is Magic', *Business Times*, 10 November 2002.

3 Koos Bekker, 'Boschkollege?', *Die Matie*, 29 August 1975.

4 Hanlie Retief, 'Die man wat die toekoms wil sien', *Rapport*, 2 March 2014.

5 *Financial Mail*, 'Read all about it!', 6 June 1984.

6 J Manuel Correia, 'Newspaper bosses keen to share TV4', *Rand Daily Mail*, 22 May 1984.

7 Ibid.

8 Lizette Rabe, *A Luta Continua: A history of media freedom in South Africa*, Stellenbosch: SUN Media, 2020, pp. 222–223.

9   Vosloo, *Across Boundaries*, p. xx.

10 Ibid. p. 29.

11 Ibid. p. 30.

12 Koos Bekker, 'Wat ek van Ton weet', in Lizette Rabe (ed.), *Ton van 'n Man*, Cape Town: NB Uitgewers, 2007.

13 Koos Bekker, 'Sakegesprek met Theo Vorster', 16 October 2012, at https://www.youtube.com/watch?v=j o9brNP2tOo&list=PLF9AXykvyZ5Pf27 unIr_m-Gz3x3zFP66P&index=6

14 Ibid.

15 Barron, 'Everything he does is Magic'.

16 CNBC Africa, 'Koos Bekker discusses his legacy & history of Naspers', 28 February 2014, at https://youtube. com/ZzMWn3JDKQs

17 Grietjie Verhoef, *The Power of Your Life: The Sanlam century of insurance empowerment, 1918–2018*, Oxford: Oxford University Press, 2018.

18 Vosloo, *Across Boundaries*, p. 30.

19 Jan Prins, 'Vriend van bodes en prinse', in Lizette Rabe (ed.), *Ton van 'n Man*.

20 Diaz Films, *Oppi Kassie*, Season 1, Episode 20, 2018.

21 Theresa Papenfus, *Pik Botha en sy Tyd*, Pretoria: Litera Publikasies, 2010, p. 755.

22 Diaz Films, *Oppi Kassie*.

23 Vosloo, *Across Boundaries*, p. 30.

24 Ibid. p. 31.

25 Arrie de Beer, author interview, 22 April 2021.

26 Vosloo, *Across Boundaries*, p. 30.

27 Papenfus, *Pik Botha en sy Tyd*, p. 756.

28 Johan de Wet, 'M-Net gaan só werk', *Beeld*, 6 September 1986.

29 Barron, 'Everything he does is Magic'.

30 Diaz Films, *Oppi Kassie*.

31 Ibid.

32 Irdeto, 'One Irdeto: Looking back moving forward', 2010, p. 16, at https://www.yumpu.com/en/ document/view/18567224/one-irdeto-looking-back-moving-forward

33 Diaz Films, *Oppi Kassie*.

34 Ibid.

35 Ibid.

36 *Financial Mail*, 'M-Net: Media success story of the 1980s', Supplement to commemorate Naspers's 75th anniversary / Naspers, 75-jaar gedenkbylaag, 20 July 1990.

37 Lizette Rabe (compiler), *'n Konstante revolusie: Naspers, Media24 en Oorgange*, Cape Town: Tafelberg, 2015.

38 Ibid.

39 Mof Terreblanche, 'Ton en 12 September 1994', in Lizette Rabe (ed.), *Ton van 'n Man*.

40 *Finansies & Tegniek*, 'Die Nasionale Pers staan sterk', 5 June 1985.

CHAPTER 3

1   Koos Bekker, Interview with Gerrie Coerts, 6 September 2014, at https://www.youtube.com/ watch?v=odMjF2jf9NE

2   Koos Bekker: 'Don't try this at home', Fin24, 11 May 2015, at https://www.news24.com/fin24/ koos-bekker-dont-try-this-at-home-20150511/

3   Chris von Ulmenstein, *SwitchBitch: My journey of transformation from*

sour to sweet, Cape Town: New Voices Publishing Services, 2018, p. 293.

4   Ibid.

5   Mark Robichaux, *Cable Cowboy: John Malone and the rise of the modern cable business*, Hoboken, New Jersey: John Wiley & Sons, 2002.

6   Andrew Halley-Wright, author interview, 27 April 2021.

7   *Beeld*, 'SAUK onder druk – Eksteen', 27 September 1986.

8   Ibid.

9   Jackie Salton, 'Pay network to have shares in TV4', *The Citizen*, 3 July 1985.

10 Ton Vosloo, *Across Boundaries: A life in the media in a time of change*, Cape Town: Jonathan Ball, 2018, p. 32.

11 Diaz Films, *Oppi Kassie*, Season 1, Episode 19, 2018.

12 Johan de Wet, 'M-Net gaan só werk ...', *Beeld*, 6 September 1986.

13 Ibid.

14 Halley-Wright, interview.

15 *Financial Mail*, 'Koos Bekker: M-inence grise of the airwaves', 31 October 1986.

16 *Business Day*, 'Vital to learn from mistakes – especially your own', Survey Entrepreneur of the Year Award, 14 October 2004.

17 Udo Rypstra, 'M-Net gets R30m loan as drive for viewers speeds up', *Sunday Times*, 22 February 1987.

18 Diaz Films, *Oppi Kassie*, Season 1, Episode 20, 2018.

19 Ibid.

20 Irdeto, 'One Irdeto', p. 30.

21 Andrew Halley-Wright, 'The making of a Lighthouse brand: How M-Net was born and bred', medium.com, 28 October 2014, at https://medium.com/@HalleyAndy/the-making-of-a-lighthouse-brand-6db505973266

22 Daleen van Wyk, 'Teaters kan maande toe staan', *Finansies & Tegniek*, 6 February 1987.

23 *Financial Mail*, 'Koos Bekker: M-inence grise of the airwaves'.

24 Daleen van Wyk, 'M-Net kry R30 miljoen by TrustBank', *Finansies & Tegniek*, 24 April 1987.

25 Thelma Tuch, 'M-Net gets R30m loan from Volkskas', *Business Day*, 27 February 1987.

26 Cobus Stofberg, quoted in Anton Harber, *Gorilla in the Room: Koos Bekker and the rise and rise of Naspers*, Johannesburg: Parktown Publishers, 2012, p. 27.

27 *Financial Mail*, 'Koos Bekker: M-inence grise of the airwaves'.

28 Douglas Gordon, 'Decoder sales zoom', *Sunday Times*, 18 December 1988.

29 De Wet, 'M-Net gaan só werk'.

30 Ibid.

31 Daleen van Wyk, 'Radio duurder as advertensie-medium', *Finansies & Tegniek*, 5 February 1988.

32 Ibid.

33 M-Net Prospectus, 2 July 1990.

34 Charlotte Mathews, 'M-Net's subscribers to get slice of R20m share issue', *Business Day*, 2 July 1990.

35 Marcia Klein, 'Decoders keep selling and expansion goes on', *Business Day*, 20 August 1992.

36 Ibid.

37 Melanie Sargeant, 'Computers and TV to "open new vistas"', *Business Day*, 21 May 1992.

38 *Finansies & Tegniek*, 'M-Net kyk na Suider-Afrika', 15 February 1991.

39 Marcia Klein, 'M-Net strikes deal with Kenyan station', *Business Day*, 18 December 1991.

40 AP-DJ, 'SA company in massive pay-TV venture', *Business Day*, 26 August 1995.

41 Ibid.

42 Ibid.

43 Ibid.

44 Harber, *Gorilla in the Room*, p. 15.

45 Vosloo, *Across Boundaries*, p. 65.

46 Julie Walker, 'Sky's the limit for M-Net', *Sunday Times*, 28 May 1995.

47 Chris Barron, 'Couch-potato chief is determined to show you some value, too', *Sunday Times* (*Business Times*), 13 April 2003.

CHAPTER 4

1 Mike Cohen, 'Naspers can buy New York Times but not interested – Bekker', Bloomberg, 17 April 2008, at https://www.moneyweb.co.za/archive/naspers-can-buy-new-york-times-but-not-interested/

2 Ton Vosloo, *Across Boundaries: A life in the media in a time of change*, Johannesburg: Jonathan Ball, 2018.

3 Koos Bekker, Address at Maastricht School of Management, Graduation Day, 9 September 2014, at https://www.youtube.com/watch?v=FP3eDRqcY24

4 Vosloo, *Across Boundaries*, pp. 167–180.

5 Sapa, 'Naspers journalists apologise for apartheid role', 26 September 1997.

6 Ibid.

7 Lizette Rabe, 'Kroniek van 'n mondigwording? 'n Mediageskiedkundige herevaluering van die WVK, Naspers en Afrikaanse joernalistiek', *LitNet Akademies*, 14(3), 2017. (Originally from W. de Kock, 'Malan meets Mandela', *Leadership* 16(4), p. 20.)

8 Mof Terreblanche, 'Ton en 12 September 1994', in Lizette Rabe (ed.), *Ton van 'n Man*, Cape Town: NB Uitgewers, 2007.

9 Ibid.

10 Vosloo, *Across Boundaries*, p. 42.

11 Terreblanche, 'Ton en 12 September 1994'.

12 *F&T Weekly*, Ton Vosloo and Koos Bekker, 'Nasionale Pers in the new world', 17 October 1997.

13 Ibid.

14 Ibid.

15 Koos Bekker, 'Swanesang vir '75', *Die Matie*, 29 August 1975.

16 Cheryl Uys-Allie, 'Corporate media entrepreneur', in *South Africa's Greatest Entrepreneurs*, compiled by Moky Mokura, Johannesburg: MME Media, 2010, p. 68.

17 CNBC Africa, 'Koos Bekker discusses his legacy & history of Naspers', 28 February 2014, at https://www.youtube.com/watch?v=ZzMWn3JDKQs

18 Tim du Plessis, 'Koerante wat nog orkane kon stook', *Rapport*, at https://www.netwerk24.com/netwerk24/stemme/menings/

tim-du-plessis-koerante-wat-nog-
orkane-kon-stook-20210404

19 Vosloo, *Across Boundaries*, p. 34.

20 Anton Harber, *Gorilla in the Room:
Koos Bekker and the rise and rise of
Naspers*, Johannesburg: Parktown
Publishers, 2012, p. 19.

21 Alec Hogg, 'Naspers annual results:
Koos Bekker – CEO, Naspers',
Moneyweb, 25 June 2008.

22 Harber, *Gorilla in the Room*, p. 18.

23 Philip de Wet, 'Technically insolvent
M-Net set to leave JSE', *This Day*,
18 December 2003.

24 Alec Hogg, 'Naspers annual results:
Koos Bekker – CEO, Naspers',
Moneyweb, 30 June 2009, at
https://www.moneyweb.co.za/
archive/naspers-results-koos-bekker-
ceo-naspers/

25 Ibid.

26 *Sunday Times* (*Business Times*),
'Land of the rising Sun',
25 September 2005.

27 S'thembiso Msomi, 'His money's
on the tokoloshe', *Sunday Times*,
10 October 2004.

28 Alec Hogg, 'Special report podcast:
Koos Bekker – CEO, Naspers',
Moneyweb, 30 November 2010,
at https://www.moneyweb.co.za/
archive/special-report-podcast-koos-
bekker-ceo-naspers-2-2/

29 David Carte, 'Naspers shocker
– growth of only 8%', Moneyweb,
29 November 2011, at
https://www.moneyweb.co.za/
archive/naspers-shocker-growth-of-
only-8/

30 Bob van Dijk, Presentation at Naspers
press conference, Johannesburg,
9 October 2019.

31 Ibid.

CHAPTER 5

1   Andrew Halley-Wright, 'The making of
a Lighthouse brand: How M-Net was
born and bred', medium.com,
28 October 2014, at https://medium.
com/@HalleyAndy/the-making-of-a-
lighthouse-brand-6db505973266

2   Chris Barron, 'Everything he does
is Magic', *Business Times*,
10 November 2002.

3   Minutes of various Eendrag house
committee meetings in 1972–1975.
Handwritten and stored in
Eendrag's archive.

4   Ibid.

5   Ibid.

6   Eendrag, Primariusverslag, 1974.

7   Ibid.

8   Jan Prins, 'Vriend van bodes en
prinse', in Lizette Rabe (ed.),
Ton van 'n Man, Cape Town:
NB Uitgewers, 2007.

9   Barron, 'Everything he does is Magic'.

10 Ibid.

11 Arrie de Beer, telephonic interview,
22 April 2021.

12 Ibid.

13 Barron, 'Everything he does is Magic'.

14 Ton Vosloo, *Across Boundaries: A life
in the media in a time of change*, Cape
Town: Jonathan Ball, 2018, p. 64.

15 *Financial Mail*, 'Koos Bekker:
M-inence grise of the airwaves',
31 October 1986.

16 Bianca Schlotterbeck, 'Silvio Berlusconi's greatest hits', CNBC, 2 October 2013, at https://www.cnbc.com/2013/10/02/Silvio-Berlusconis-greatest-hits.html

17 Anton Harber, *Gorilla in the Room: Koos Bekker and the rise and rise of Naspers*, Johannesburg: Parktown Publishers, 2012, p. 27.

18 Luke Alfred, 'Unlikely team comes together to save SA bid', *Sunday Times*, 16 May 2004.

19 Ibid.

20 Halley-Wright, 'The making of a Lighthouse brand'.

21 Toby Shapshak, 'Money and the box', *Financial Mail*, 24–30 November 2016.

22 Ibid.

23 Alec Hogg, 'Special Report Podcast: Koos Bekker – CEO, Naspers', Moneyweb, 27 January 2012, at https://www.moneyweb.co.za/archive/special-report-podcast-koos-bekker-ceo-naspers-6/

24 News24, 'Naspers apologises for its role in apartheid', 25 July 2015, at https://www.news24.com/News24/Naspers-apologises-for-its-role-in-apartheid-20150725

25 Diaz Films, *Oppi Kassie*, Season 2, Episode 1, 2019.

26 Ebbe Dommisse, *Fortunes: The rise and rise of Afrikaner tycoons*, Johannesburg: Jonathan Ball, 2021, p. 64.

27 TJ Strydom, 'SA doesn't want our dollars – Naspers', *Sunday Times*, 25 August 2019. (author attended meeting).

28 Marelize Barnard, 'MultiChoice wou TV-projek kaap, sê Carrim voor Zondo', Netwerk24, 25 February 2020, at https://www.netwerk24.com/netwerk24/nuus/politiek/multichoice-wou-tv-projek-kaap-se-carrim-voor-zondo-20200225

29 Rob Rose, 'Davies' confidence trick revives sunshine agenda', *Sunday Times*, 21 June 2015

CHAPTER 6

1 Anton Harber, *Gorilla in the Room: Koos Bekker and the rise and rise of Naspers*, Johannesburg: Parktown Publishers, 2012.

2 Koos Bekker, 'From farmer's son to global digital success', Interview with Hanna Ziady, Moneyweb, 25 February 2016, at https://www.moneyweb.co.za/moneyweb-radio/from-farmers-son-to-global-digital-success/

3 Leng Hu, *Ma Huateng and Tencent: A biography of one of China's greatest entrepreneurs*, London: LID Publishing, Kindle Edition, 2017.

4 Rachel Duffell, 'A look at Pony Ma's meteoric rise', Gen.T, 21 October 2018, at https://generationt.asia/leaders/a-look-at-pony-mas-meteoric-rise

5 TJ Strydom, 'Crushed by the golden goose', *Financial Mail*, 20–26 May 2021.

6 Ton Vosloo, *Across Boundaries: A life in the media in a time of change*, Cape Town: Jonathan Ball, 2018, p. 47.

7 Strydom, 'Crushed by the golden goose'.

8 Vosloo, *Across Boundaries*, p. 49.

9   Ibid., p. 50.

10   Hans Hawinkels, author interview, 15 March 2021.

11   Duncan MacLeod, 'Antonie Roux: Attracting eyeballs', *Financial Mail*, 6 October 2006.

12   Vosloo, *Across Boundaries*, p. 46.

13   Hawinkels, interview.

14   Vosloo, *Across Boundaries*, p. 55.

15   CNBC Africa, 'Koos Bekker discusses his legacy and the history of Naspers', 28 February 2014, at https://youtube.com/ZzMWn3JDKQs

16   Alec Hogg, 'TMT Slot: Naspers interim results. Koos Bekker – CEO, Naspers', Moneyweb, 26 November 2009, at https://www.moneyweb.co.za/archive/tmt-slot-naspers-interim-results-koos-bekker-ceo/

17   Themba Hlengani, 'Just watch it grow', *Financial Mail*, 6 October 2006.

18   Lindsay Williams, 'Fancy decoders and virtual kittens give Naspers a lift', *Business Day*, 30 November 2005 (transcript of interview on Summit TV).

19   Hogg, 'TMT slot'.

20   Alec Hogg, 'Special report podcast: Koos Bekker – CEO, Naspers', Moneyweb, 27 June 2012, at https://www.moneyweb.co.za/archive/special-report-podcast-koos-bekker-ceo-naspers-7/

21   MacLeod, 'Attracting eyeballs'.

22   Ibid.

23   Hogg, 'Special report podcast'.

24   Harber, *Gorilla in the Room*.

25   Julie Walker, 'After OpenTV, MIHH needs a little openness', *Sunday Times*, 7 March 1999.

26   David Carte, 'What Koos Bekker learnt on holiday', Moneyweb, 11 April 2008.

27   Byron Kennedy , 'Koos Bekker: CEO Naspers', Moneyweb extract from CNBC Africa's Power Lunch, 11 April 2008, at https://www.moneyweb.co.za/archive/koos-bekker-ceo-naspers-9/

28   Ibid.

29   Hogg, 'Special report podcast'.

30   Basil Sgourdos, author interview, 12 May 2021.

CHAPTER 7

1   Alec Hogg, 'Bonanza from China', Moneyweb, 26 November 2009, at https://www.moneyweb.co.za/archive/bonanza-from-china/

2   Alec Hogg, 'Davos 2010: Koos Bekker, CEO of Naspers', Moneyweb, 27 January 2010 at https://www.moneyweb.co.za/archive/perspectives-on-davos-koos-bekker-ceo-naspers/

3   Sasha Planting, 'Koos the dragon-slayer', Moneyweb, 25 August 2017, at https://www.moneyweb.co.za/news/companies-and-deals/koos-the-dragon-slayer/

4   Terzah Ewing, 'Merrill Lynch scores again with IPOs after a slow start', *Wall Street Journal*, 24 November 1999, at https://www.wsj.com/articles/SB943395221860295520

5   Kara Swisher, 'OpenTV to buy web pioneer Spyglass for $2.5 billion in an all-stock deal', *Wall Street Journal*, 27 March 2000, at https://www.wsj.com/articles/SB954111665747755832

6   *Financial Mail*, 'A smaller slice of the ad spend cake', Top Companies Supplement, 29 June 2001.

7   Liberty Media Corporation, Annual Report, April 2004.

8   Lindsay Williams, 'Fancy decoders and virtual kittens give Naspers a lift', *Business Day*, 30 November 2005 (transcript of interview on Summit TV).

9   Alec Hogg, 'Special report podcast: Koos Bekker – CEO, Naspers', 27 November 2009, at https://www.moneyweb.co.za/archive/moneyweb-special-report-podcast-koos-bekker-ceo-n/

10 Ibid.

11 Hilton Tarrant, 'Koos Bekker: DStv's competitor won't come from satellite-based TV', Moneyweb, 27 November 2012, at https://www.moneyweb.co.za/archive/koos-bekker-dstvs-competitor-wont-come-from-satell/

12 Woolworths Holdings Limited, 2014 Integrated Report, at https://www.woolworthsholdings.co.za/wp-content/uploads/2017/12/whl_2014_integrated_reprt1.pdf

13 Reuters, 'Tiger Brands to sell stake in Nigerian unit to Dangote Industries', 14 December 2015, at https://www.reuters.com/article/tiger-brands-divestiture-dangote-industr-idUSL3N14327T20151214

14 Bojosi Morule and Daan Steenkamp, 'The structure of South Africa's external position', *Occasional Bulletin of Economic Notes*, OBEN/18/02, September 2018.

15 Alec Hogg, 'Special report podcast: Koos Bekker – CEO, Naspers', Moneyweb, 27 June 2011, at https://www.moneyweb.co.za/archive/special-report-podcast-koos-bekker-ceo-naspers-4/

16 Planting, 'Koos the dragon-slayer'.

17 Ibid.

18 Hogg, 'Bonanza from China'.

19 Duncan MacLeod, 'Antonie Roux: Attracting eyeballs', *Financial Mail*, 6 October 2006.

20 Basil Sgourdos, author interview, 12 May 2021.

21 Alec Hogg, 'Cobus Stofberg: Acting CEO Naspers', Moneyweb, 27 November 2007, at https://www.moneyweb.co.za/archive/cobus-stofberg-acting-ceo-naspers/

22 Hogg, 'Special report podcast', 27 June 2011.

23 Kevin Mattison, author interview, 18 May 2021. Comments also published in TJ Strydom, 'Crushed by the golden goose', *Financial Mail*, 20–26 May 2021.

CHAPTER 8

1   'E&Y World Entrepreneur global awards: Koos Bekker: CEO, Naspers', Moneyweb, 27 May 2008, at https://www.moneyweb.co.za/archive/ey-world-entrepreneur-global-awards-koos-bekker-ce/

2   Koos Bekker, Interview with Gerrie Coerts, 6 September 2014, at https://www.youtube.com/watch?v=odMjF2jf9NE

3   Johan de Wet, 'M-Net gaan só werk ...', *Beeld*, 6 September 1986.

4   Plum Productions, MultiChoice Heritage Video, 2015.

5   De Wet, 'M-Net gaan só werk ...'

6   MultiChoice Heritage Video.

7   Ton Vosloo, *Across Boundaries: A life in the media in a time of change*, Johannesburg: Jonathan Ball, 2018, p. 43.

8   Chris Barron, 'Everything he does is Magic', *Business Times*, 10 November 2002.

9   MultiChoice Heritage Video.

10 Anton Harber, *Gorilla in the Room: Koos Bekker and the rise and rise of Naspers*, Johannesburg: Parktown Publishers, 2012, p. 25.

11 Hennie van Deventer, *Laatoes: Kykweer van 'n kanniedood-koerantman*, Gansbaai: Naledi, 2017, p. 40.

12 Ibid. p. 41.

13 Matthew Buckland, *So You Want to Build a Startup?*, Cape Town: Tafelberg, 2019.

14 Esmaré Weideman, 'Tiaras, trane en tee – tien jaar by Huisgenoot, You en Drum', in Lizette Rabe (compiler), *'n Konstante revolusie: Naspers, Media24 en oorgange*, Cape Town: Tafelberg, 2015.

15 Vosloo, *Across Boundaries*, p. 64.

16 Bekker, Interview with Gerrie Coerts.

17 Harber, *Gorilla in the Room*, pp. 11–12.

18 Ibid.

19 Ibid. p. 25.

20 Hilton Tarrant, 'Upper echelon: Lehlohonolo Letele – executive chairman of MultiChoice', Moneyweb, 12 December 2012, at https://www.moneyweb.co.za/archive/upper-echelon-lehlohonolo-letele-executive-chairm/

21 Buckland, *So You Want to Build a Startup?*, p. 115.

22 Koos Bekker, Address at Maastricht School of Management, Graduation Day, 9 September 2014, at https://www.youtube.com/watch?v=FP3eDRqcY24

23 Hanlie Retief, 'Die man wat die toekoms wil sien', *Rapport*, 2 March 2014.

24 Koos Bekker, Address at Maastricht School of Management.

25 Buckland, *So You Want to Build a Startup?*, p. 115.

26 Ron Derby, 'Naspers' BEE plans exclude A-shares', *Business Day*, 7 February 2006.

27 Koos Bekker receiving Entrepreneur of the Year Award, copy of speech in Hermann Giliomee correspondence, Africana collection, Stellenbosch University Library, 2006.

28 Chris Buchanan, 'Koos Bekker: CEO, Naspers – extract from today's interview on CNBC Africa's Power Lunch in association with Moneyweb', 11 April 2008, at https://www.moneyweb.co.za/archive/koos-bekker-ceo-naspers-9/

29 Giulietta Talevi, 'Naspers chief to go on leave, but business continues as usual', *Business Day*, 15 November 2006 (transcript of interview on Summit TV).

30 Buchanan, 'Koos Bekker: CEO, Naspers'.

CHAPTER 9

1 *Financial Mail*, 'Financial democracy and the lesson of Naspers', 3 February 2006.
2 Jannie Mouton, *'En toe fire hulle my'*, Cape Town: Tafelberg, 2011, p. 108 (translated).
3 Mouton, *'En toe fire hulle my'*.
4 Ibid. p. 53.
5 Ibid. p. 107.
6 Ton Vosloo, *Across Boundaries: A life in the media in a time of change*, Johannesburg: Jonathan Ball, 2018, p. 42.
7 Mouton, *'En toe fire hulle my'*, p. 95.
8 Bloomberg, 'No let-up in PSG takeover bid for Keeromstraat', *Business Day*, 5 January 2006.
9 Ibid.
10 Vosloo, *Across Boundaries*, pp. 39–40.
11 Adele Shevel, 'Board has iron grip on Naspers', *Business Times*, 29 January 2006.
12 Fin24, 'The battle of Keeromstraat', 26 January 2006.
13 Ibid.
14 Ebbe Dommisse, *Fortunes: The rise and rise of Afrikaner tycoons* Johannesburg: Jonathan Ball, 2017.
15 Ibid.
16 Ron Derby, 'Sanlam heads off PSG battle over Naspers', *Business Day*, 27 January 2006.
17 Vosloo, *Across Boundaries*, p. 71.
18 Shevel, 'Board has iron grip on Naspers'.
19 Mouton, *'En toe fire hulle my'*, p. 79.

CHAPTER 10

1 Hanlie Retief, 'Die man wat die toekoms wil sien', *Rapport*, 2 March 2014.
2 Ton Vosloo, *Across Boundaries: A life in the media in a time of change*, Johannesburg: Jonathan Ball, 2018, p. 65.
3 Toby Shapshak, 'Money and the box', *Financial Mail*, 24–30 November 2016.
4 Ibid.
5 Ibid.
6 Retief, 'Die man wat die toekoms wil sien'.
7 Giulietta Talevi and Rob Rose, 'Nooit, China! Why Koos Bekker won't be selling Tencent anytime soon', *Financial Mail*, 31 Aug.–6 Sept. 2017.
8 Koos Bekker, 'We have two choices: Diversity or claustrophobia', *Sunday Times*, 10 November 2002.
9 Vosloo, *Across Boundaries*, p. 48.
10 Ibid.
11 Alec Hogg, 'Naspers interim results: Koos Bekker – CEO, Naspers', Moneyweb, 26 November 2008, at https://www.moneyweb.co.za/archive/naspers-interim-results-koos-bekker-ceo-naspers/
12 Bekker, 'We have two choices'.
13 Talevi and Rose, 'Nooit, China!'
14 Cheryl Uys-Allie, 'Corporate media entrepreneur', in *South Africa's Greatest Entrepreneurs*, compiled by Moky Mokura, Johannnesburg: MME Media, 2010, p. 68.
15 Retief, 'Die man wat die toekoms wil sien'.

16 Alec Hogg, 'Special report podcast: Koos Bekker – CEO, Naspers', Moneyweb, 27 June 2011, at https://www.moneyweb.co.za/archive/special-report-podcast-koos-bekker-ceo-naspers-4/

17 Megan Davies, 'Russia's Mail.Ru sells remaining Facebook stock', Reuters, 5 September 2013, at https://www.reuters.com/article/us-mailru-results-idUSBRE98409720130905

18 Hilton Tarrant, 'Koos Bekker: DStv's competitor won't come from satellite-based TV', Moneyweb, 27 November 2012, at https://www.moneyweb.co.za/archive/koos-bekker-dstvs-competitor-wont-come-from-satell/

19 Alec Hogg, 'Special report podcast: Koos Bekker – CEO, Naspers', Moneyweb, 30 November 2010, at https://www.moneyweb.co.za/archive/naspers-fullyear-results-koos-bekker-ceo-naspers/

20 Vosloo, *Across Boundaries*, p. 54.

21 Hans Hawinkels, author interview, 15 March 2021.

22 *Business Day Africa*, 'SA Media group's foray into Brazil', 12 May 2006.

23 Vosloo, *Across Boundaries*, p. 47.

24 Leena Rao, 'Naspers leads $17 million round in private sales site Brandsclub', Techcrunch, 17 May 2010, at https://techcrunch.com/2010/05/17/naspers-leads-17-million-round-in-private-sales-site-brandsclub/

25 Takealot, 'Kalahari merges with takealot.com: Two of South Africa's leading eCommerce businesses combine to create a platform of scale', media release, 7 October 2014, at https://www.takealot.com/company-news/kalahari-merges-with-takealot-com

26 Naspers, Annual Report, 2020.

27 Vosloo, *Across Boundaries*, p. 64.

CHAPTER 11

1 Sasha Planting, 'Koos the dragon-slayer', Moneyweb, 25 August 2017, at https://www.moneyweb.co.za/news/companies-and-deals/koos-the-dragon-slayer/

2 University of Cambridge Judge Business School, The Cadbury Archive, at http://cadbury.cjbs.archios.info/report

3 *The Guardian*, 'Ghislaine Maxwell to be sentenced in New York in late June', 15 January 2022, at https://www.theguardian.com/us-news/2022/jan/15/ghislaine-maxwell-to-be-sentenced-in-new-york-in-late-june

4 University of Cambridge Judge Business School, The Cadbury Archive, at https://www.jbs.cam.ac.uk/faculty-research/cadbury-archive/

5 *Business Report*, 'The Masterbond saga: 1983–2005', 20 March 2005, at https://www.iol.co.za/business-report/economy/the-masterbond-saga-1983-2005-750067

6 *Financial Mail*, 'Upturning economics', 31 August–6 September 2017.

7 Institute of Directors South Africa (IoDSA), *King Report on Corporate Governance in SA*, at https://www.iodsa.co.za/page/kingIII

8   Renelle Naidoo, 'Mandela flexed muscle to have Virgin save H&R', IOL, 16 December 2000, at https://www.iol.co.za/news/south-africa/mandela-flexed-muscle-to-have-virgin-save-h-and-r-56699

9   Moneyweb, 'Koos Bekker: CEO Naspers' – extract from today's interview on CNBC Africa's Power Lunch', 11 April 2008, at https://www.moneyweb.co.za/archive/koos-bekker-ceo-naspers-9/

10   Ibid.

11   Moneyweb, 'Koos Bekker vs Yunus Carrim', 4 December 2017, at https://www.moneyweb.co.za/news/companies-and-deals/probe-naspers-and-multichoice/

12   Jaques Pauw, *The President's Keepers: Those keeping Zuma in power and out of prison*, Cape Town: Tafelberg, 2017.

13   Giulietta Talevi, 'Koos in the firing line: Come clean, Carrim tells Koos', *Financial Mail*, 7 December 2017.

14   News24, 'SABC-MultiChoice deal: Were old shows worth R533m?', 5 October 2015, at https://www.news24.com/News24/SABC-MultiChoice-deal-Were-old-shows-worth-R533m-20151005

15   Jan Vermeulen, 'The contract MultiChoice signed with ANN7 for R50 million per year', My Broadband, 14 November 2017, at https://mybroadband.co.za/news/broadcasting/237322-the-contract-multichoice-signed-with-ann7-for-r50-million-per-year.html

16   Philip de Wet, 'ANN7 sacrificed to save MultiChoice "mistake men"', *Mail & Guardian*, 1 February 2018 at https://mg.co.za/article/2018-02-01-ann7-sacrificed-to-save-multichoice-mistake/ and Rebecca Davis, 'MultiChoice and ANN7: So many questions still left unanswered', *Daily Maverick*, 1 February 2018 at https://www.dailymaverick.co.za/article/2018-02-01-multichoice-and-ann7-so-many-questions-still-left-unanswered/.

17   Vermeulen, 'The contract MultiChoice signed with ANN7'.

18   Ibid.

19   Planting, 'Koos the dragon-slayer'.

20   *Financial Mail*, 'Upturning economics'.

21   Ann Crotty, 'Naspers pay policy gets thumbs down', *Business Day*, 28 August 2017.

22   Giulietta Talevi, 'Investors to tackle Koos Bekker over Naspers pay policy', *Business Day*, 21 August 2017, at https://www.businesslive.co.za/bd/companies/2017-08-21-investors-to-tackle-koos-bekker-over-naspers-pay-policy/

23   Marc Hasenfuss, 'Bekker closes pay talk. "I've ruled. The end"', *Sunday Times*, 27 August 2017.

24   Andile Khumalo, 'Of governance, games and washing hands', *Sunday Times*, 10 September 2017.

25   Lameez Omarjee, 'Naspers-Prosus share swap done and dusted', Fin24, 16 August 2021, at https://www.news24.com/fin24/companies/naspers-prosus-share-swap-done-and-dusted-20210816

26 Ton Vosloo, *Across Boundaries: A life in the media in a time of change*, Cape Town: Jonathan Ball, 2018, p. 36.

27 *Financial Mail*, 'Upturning economics'.

CHAPTER 12

1 *Financial Mail*, 'Koos Bekker: M-inence grise of the airwaves', 31 October 1986.

2 Paul Dobson, 'Contemporary backs die', Rugby365, 2 February 2013, at https://rugby365.com/laws-referees/news/contemporary-backs-die/

3 *Beeld*, 'WP-vleuel red babatjie uit vlamme', 26 January 1988.

4 Ton Vosloo, *Across Boundaries: A life in the media in a time of change*, Johannesburg: Jonathan Ball, 2018.

5 Richard Kay, 'The Newt that almost sank Britain's glorious new garden: How one tiny visitor delayed a visionary £50million renovation of the grounds of Somerset's most beautiful mansion', *The Daily Mail*, 8 June 2019 at https://www.dailymail.co.uk/news/article-7118195/The-Newt-sank-Britains-glorious-new-garden.html

6 *Financial Mail*, 'Koos Bekker: M-inence grise of the airwaves'.

7 *Rand Daily Mail*, 'Last night's viewing', PlayMail, 10 June 1976.

8 *Sunday Times*, 'Dream banquet honours tycoons', 10 November 2002.

9 Koos Bekker, Address at Maastricht School of Management, Graduation Day, 9 September 2014, at https://www.youtube.com/watch?v=FP3eDRqcY24

10 PC Swanepoel, *Really Inside BOSS: A tale of South Africa's late intelligence service (and something about the CIA)*, 2007, pp. 52–53.

11 Maritz Spaarwater, *A Spook's Progress: From making war to making peace*, Cape Town: Zebra Press, 2012.

12 Niël Barnard, with Tobie Wiese, *Peaceful Revolution: Inside the war room at the negotiations*, Cape Town: Tafelberg, 2017.

13 Gus Silber, '1987: Who will make us glad? Who will make us mad?', *Sunday Times*, 11 January 1987.

14 Toby Shapshak, 'Money and the box', *Financial Mail*, 24–30 November 2016.

15 CNBC Africa, 28 February 2014, at https://youtube.com/ZzMWn3JDKQs

16 Paul Martin, 'SA makes its final cup bid', *Business Day*, 6 July 2000.

17 Koos Bekker, 'Overcoming the victim mentality', *City Press*, 18 July 2010.

18 *Fortune*, YouTube channel, 'Africa: The new frontier for economic growth at the Global Forum 2010', 31 July 2014, at https://www.youtube.com/watch?v=H4vMfXb_ojQ

19 Gabriël J Botma, '"Koos sê ...": 'n Kritiese diskoersanalise van die metakapitaal van 'n invloedryke Suid-Afrikaanse mediamagnaat', *Tydskrif vir Geesteswetenskappe* 56(1), 2016.

20 Koos Bekker, 'Turbulence after Covid-19 will force SA either right or left', 10 May 2020, at https://www.news24.com/news24/Analysis/koos-bekker-turbulence-after-covid-19-will-force-sa-either-right-or-left-20200507

21 Bob van Dijk, author interview,
    12 July 2021.

CHAPTER 13

1   Koos Bekker, Acceptance speech, Ernst
    & Young Entrepreneur of the Year
    Award, 2006, transcript forms part of
    correspondence between Bekker and
    Hermann Giliomee, accessed through
    Stellenbosch University Library's
    Africana Collection.

2   Naspers Annual General Meeting,
    25 August 2021, author's own
    transcript from webcast accessed live
    via Naspers weblink.

3   Alec Hogg, 'Naspers shrugs off Google's
    Chinese fight', Moneyweb, 13 January
    2010, at https://www.moneyweb.
    co.za/archive/naspers-shrugs-off-
    googles-chinese-fight/

4   Alec Hogg, 'Special report podcast:
    Koos Bekker – CEO, Naspers',
    Moneyweb, 30 November 2010, at
    https://www.moneyweb.co.za/
    archive/special-report-podcast-koos-
    bekker-ceo-naspers-2-2/

5   Human Rights Watch, 'Russia:
    Social media pressured to censor
    posts', 5 February 2021, at
    https://www.hrw.org/
    news/2021/02/05/russia-social-
    media-pressured-censor-posts

6   Caitlin Thompson and Masho
    Lomashvili, 'Russians face
    grim options on social media',
    Coda, 3 April 2022, at
    https://www.codastory.com/
    authoritarian-tech/russia-vkontakte-
    censorship/

7   Human Rights Watch, 'Russia-Ukraine
    war', at https://www.hrw.org/tag/
    russia-ukraine-war?promo=tag

8   Jake Rudnitsky and Irina Reznik,
    'Son of Putin aide named head
    of Russia's top social network',
    Bloomberg, 13 December 2021, at
    https://www.bloomberg.com/news/
    articles/2021-12-13/son-of-putin-aide-
    named-head-of-russia-s-leading-
    social-network

9   Prosus NV/Naspers business update,
    'War in Ukraine', 7 March 2022, at
    https://presspage-production-content.
    s3.amazonaws.com/
    uploads/2658/2022-03-
    0741948prosusnvinvestorcall.
    mp3?10000

10 Naspers, Integrated Annual Report,
    2014.

11 Chris Buchanan, 'Koos Bekker:
    CEO Naspers' – extract from today's
    interview at CNBC Africa Power
    Lunch in association with
    Moneyweb', 11 April 2008, at
    https://www.moneyweb.co.za/
    archive/koos-bekker-ceo-naspers-9/

12 Tiisetso Motsoeneng, 'Naspers
    buys ad website from Gumtree
    founders', 3 October 2011,
    at https://www.reuters.com/
    article/naspers-
    idUKL5E7L309Y20111003

13 Prosus NV/Naspers business update,
    'War in Ukraine'.

14 Prosus, 'Statement on Avito',
    25 March 2022, at
    https://www.prosus.com/news/
    statement-on-avito/

15 Prosus, 'Prosus to sell its shareholding in Avito', 20 May 2022, at https://www.prosus.com/news/statement-on-avito/

16 Naspers Integrated Annual Report, 2015.

17 Alec Hogg, 'Special report podcast: Koos Bekker – CEO, Naspers', Moneyweb, 27 June 2012, at https://www.moneyweb.co.za/archive/special-report-podcast-koos-bekker-ceo-naspers-6/

18 In a communist state, the Politburo is, of course, the highest authority.

19 Charles Searle, response to a shareholder question at Naspers AGM, 25 August 2021, webcast accessed live via Naspers weblink.

20 Ibid.

21 Ibid.

22 Ibid.

23 Naspers Annual General Meeting, 25 August 2021.

24 Ibid.

25 T.J. Strydom, 'Bob van Dijk unfazed by Beijing's tech crackdown', *Financial Mail*, 15 July 2021.

26 Yvonne Lau, 'The year since Beijing canceled the world's biggest IPO is proof that the golden era of Chinese listings is gone for good', *Fortune*, 3 November 2021, at https://fortune.com/2021/11/03/one-year-after-suspended-ant-ipo-alibaba-china-tech-crackdown-overseas-listings/

27 Nian Liu, Yuan Yang, Ryan McMorrow and Sun Yu, 'Tencent takes quiet path through China's tech turbulence', *Financial Times*, 24 June 2021, at ft.com/content/97d8395b-6115-4147-b4d8-953ddbf729a4

28 Jamil Anderlini, 'Under Xi Jinping, China is turning back to dictatorship', *Financial Times*, 11 October 2017.

29 Hogg, 'Naspers shrugs off Google's Chinese fight'.

30 Anton Harber, *Gorilla in the Room: Koos Bekker and the rise and rise of Naspers*, Johannesburg: Parktown Publishers, 2012, p. 37.

CHAPTER 14

1 Geoff Candy, 'Koos Bekker on entrepreneurship', Moneyweb, 7 June 2007, at https://www.moneyweb.co.za/archive/koos-bekker-on-entrepreneurship/

2 *Hannes aan Huis* – Koos Bekker, kykNET, 14 April 2021, at https://www.facebook.com/kykNET

3 Cheryl Uys-Allie, 'Corporate media entrepreneur', in *South Africa's Greatest Entrepreneurs*, compiled by Moky Mokura, Johannesburg: MME Media, 2010, p. 59.

4 Ibid.

5 Hanlie Retief, 'Die man wat die toekoms wil sien', *Rapport*, 2 March 2014.

6 Gerard van Niekerk, 'Die man wat jou vrye tyd wil hê', *De Kat*, July 1990.

7 Maggs on Media / Koos Bekker, Part 1, 22 August 2014, at https://www.youtube.com/watch?v=R8DDrZ6uZ1M&t=1s

8   Uys-Allie, 'Corporate media entrepreneur', p. 61.

9   *Hannes aan Huis* – Koos Bekker.

10 Chris Barron, 'Everything he does is Magic', *Business Times*, 10 November 2002.

11 Lindsay Williams, 'Koos Bekker discusses his legacy & history of Naspers', CNBC Africa, 28 February 2014, at https://www.youtube.com/watch?v=ZzMWn3JDKQs

12 Caroline Gibbs, *10 Years of Cellular Freedom*, MTN Group Corporate Affairs, 2004.

13 Ton Vosloo, *Across Boundaries: A life in South African media in a time of change*, Johannesburg: Jonathan Ball, 2018, p. 33.

14 Shaun Harris, 'MultiChoice still speculative', *Financial Mail*, 23 June 1995.

15 Johann Rupert, 'No desire for revenge', *Business Day*, 11 September 2013.

16 David Meades, *Afrikaner-Kapitalisme: Van brandarm tot stinkryk*, Gansbaai: Naledi, 2019, p. 262.

17 Ibid.

18 Uys-Allie, 'Corporate media entrepreneur', p. 65.

19 Jo Johnson and Martine Orange, *The Man Who Tried to Buy the World: Jean-Marie Messier and Vivendi Universal*, New York: Viking, 2003.

20 Ebbe Dommisse, *Fortunes: The rise and rise of Afrikaner tycoons*, Johannesburg: Jonathan Ball, 2021, p. 46.

21 Prosus. ecommerce portfolio factsheet, November 2021, at https://presspage-production-content.s3.amazonaws.com/uploads/2658/prosussegment-factsheets22november.pdf?10000

22 Lizette Rabe (ed.), *Ton van 'n Man*, Cape Town: NB Uitgewers, 2007.

CHAPTER 15

1   Charles Darwin, *The Origin of Species*, 2009 edition, London: Vintage, p. 670.

2   Anton Harber, *Gorilla in the Room: Koos Bekker and the rise and rise of Naspers*, Johannesburg: Parktown Publishers, 2012, p. 25.

3   Ebbe Dommisse, *Fortunes: The rise and rise of Afrikaner tycoons* Johannesburg: Jonathan Ball, 2021, p. 75.

4   *Financial Mail*, 'Koos Bekker: M-inence grise of the airwaves', 31 October 1986.

5   Harber, *Gorilla in the Room,* p. 20.

6   Maggs on Media / Koos Bekker, Part 3, 22 August 2014, at https://www.youtube.com/watch?v=epMvBAMTDjk

7   Alec Hogg, 'TMT slot: Naspers interim results. Koos Bekker – CEO, Naspers', Moneyweb, 26 November 2009, at https://www.moneyweb.co.za/archive/tmt-slot-naspers-interim-results-koos-bekker-ceo/

8   Maggs on Media / Koos Bekker, Part 3.

9   Hogg, 'Naspers interim results'.

10 Maggs on Media / Koos Bekker, Part 3.

11 Chantelle Benjamin, 'Naspers: Well-read in bouncing back from bad ventures', *Business Day*, 16 October 2009.

12   Cheryl Uys-Allie, 'Corporate media
     entrepreneur', in *South Africa's
     Greatest Entrepreneurs*, compiled by
     Moky Mokura, Johannesburg:
     MME Media, 2010, p. 68.

13   Maggs on Media / Koos Bekker,
     Part 1, 22 August 2014,
     at https://www.youtube.com/
     watch?v=R8DDrZ6uZ1M

14   Alec Hogg, 'Naspers annual results:
     Koos Bekker – CEO, Naspers',
     Moneyweb, 25 June 2008,
     at https://www.moneyweb.co.za/
     archive/naspers-annual-results-koos-
     bekker-ceo-naspers/

15   Larry Illg, author interview,
     19 July 2021.

16   Pieter Hundersmarck, author
     interview, 17 September 2021.

17   Ibid.

18   Neelash Hansjee, author interview,
     7 September 2021.

19   Lindsay Williams, 'Koos Bekker
     discusses his legacy & history
     of Naspers', CNBC Africa,
     28 February 2014,
     at https://www.youtube.com/
     watch?v=ZzMWn3JDKQs

20   Alec Hogg, 'Naspers results:
     Koos Bekker – CEO, Naspers',
     Moneyweb, 30 June 2009, at
     https://www.moneyweb.co.za/
     archive/naspers-results-koos-bekker-
     ceo-naspers/

21   Hanlie Retief, 'Die man wat die
     toekoms wil sien', *Rapport*,
     2 March 2014.

22   Williams, 'Koos Bekker discusses his
     legacy & history of Naspers'.

AFTERWORD

1   TJ Strydom, 'Going Dutch on Naspers',
     Sunday Times, 31 March 2019.